EVERYDAY PRAYERS — FOR — GENTLENESS

EVERYDAY PRAYERS
— FOR —
GENTLENESS

Embracing the Quiet Strength of Tenderness

CHRISTIE THOMAS

WHITAKER HOUSE

Everyday Prayers for Gentleness
Embracing the Radical Strength of Tenderness

littleshootsdeeproots.com

ISBN: 979-8-88769-610-2 | eBook ISBN: 979-8-88769-611-9
Printed in Colombia

Whitaker House | 1030 Hunt Valley Circle | New Kensington, PA 15068
www.whitakerhouse.com

Library of Congress Cataloging-in-Publication Data
Names: Thomas, Christie author
Title: Everyday prayers for gentleness : embracing the radical strength of tenderness / Christie Thomas.
Description: New Kensington, PA : Whitaker House, [2026] | Summary: "A devotional and reflective journal written especially for women that uses Scripture readings to pray to God, designed to help readers view Christlike gentleness not as a weakness but as a strength empowered by the Holy Spirit"— Provided by publisher.
Identifiers: LCCN 2025033513 (print) | LCCN 2025033514 (ebook) | ISBN 9798887696102 trade paperback | ISBN 9798887696119 ebook
Subjects: LCSH: Women—Prayers and devotions | Women—Religious aspects—Christianity | BISAC: RELIGION / Christian Living / Devotional Journal | RELIGION / Christian Living / Devotional
Classification: LCC BV4844 .T466 2026 (print) | LCC BV4844 (ebook)
LC record available at https://lccn.loc.gov/2025033513
LC ebook record available at https://lccn.loc.gov/2025033514

1 2 3 4 5 6 7 8 9 10 11 **ᴡʜ** 33 32 31 30 29 28 27 26

CONTENTS

Foreword 7
Introduction 10
1. How to Hold a Baby 13
2. He Is Strong 17
3. The Father Heart of God 21
4. God's Response to Our Sin 25
5. God's Response to Our Weakness 29
6. The Good Shepherd 33
7. The Lion and the Lamb 37
8. Master of Angels 41
9. Gentle and Lowly in Heart 46
10. The Gentle Partner 50
11. Alive with Gentleness 54
12. Fruitful Gentleness 58
13. Pursuing Gentleness 62
14. Putting on Gentleness 66
15. Practicing Gentleness 71
16. Just Enough Power 75
17. Gentleness in Criticism 80
18. Resisting Gently 85
19. Vengeance Is the Lord's 89

20. Trusting Meekness 94
21. Gentle Leadership 98
22. Biting and Devouring 102
23. Gentle Evangelism 107
24. Gentle Tongues 111
25. Gentle Wisdom 115
26. Gentleness and Humility 120
27. Gentleness and Anger 125
28. Gentleness and Justice 130
29. Gentleness and Beauty 134
30. Gentleness and Warfare 139
About the Author 144

FOREWORD

He's five, and he's scared to go to school. And she learns of this through my blog, where I'm calling on mothers to pray, and she prays, yes, but more than this, Christie Thomas writes a story for my boy.

She writes about an owl who is scared, and this owl's father teaches him to tuck a stone beneath his wing to remember God, the unchanging Rock. And because of this powerful word, my boy begins to tuck a stone inside his pocket. Whenever he's at preschool and scared, his little fingers reach inside his pocket, touch the smooth side of the stone, and he knows God is with him.

Much like David with his sling and five stones, the gentleness of a story can be misunderstood, something to mock—words, stones, in the face of giants?

Yet God spoke, and there was light. In the beginning was the Word and the Word was with God, tucked inside Elohim like a stone inside a little boy's jean pocket. Is there any place more powerful than "with God"?

The world mocks, even as Goliath and David's own brothers, and yet. They were silent when the stone found its target.

Because gentleness is a sheath, and inside it is the Word, which is the sharpest of weapons, living and active, and gentleness carries it, softly, tenderly.

Gentleness is that little boy's pocket, is the wing of El Shaddai, is the cleft in the rock Elijah ran to.

For he ran, as we all do, from Jezebel and Ahab and the callous laughter of an unrestrained world.

He fled it all, and God tucked him into the cleft of a rock, said, "Listen." And into the empty, worn-out soul of a prophet wondering if any soft place was left to fall, came the Word.

There was the hurricane, of course, and the fire, and the earthquake, and these were all of God, too, created by Him, but they were not *Him*. They were simply His potential. Because gentleness is but weakness if not character reined in.

These natural displays and earthly rumblings were all the crescendo leading up to the solo which was the quietest, sweetest, most musical of notes—God's whisper.

A pure reining in of power, this, like all the sinews and muscles of a horse, stilled, in submission to the greater good. The good of His people.

This is gentleness, and this is my friend Christie.

I can still see her, kneeling on the snowy sidewalk. It was Christmas, this past year, and it was cold and we were downtown, handing out Bibles and blankets and coffee. I'd hurried past someone. Stopped to give them a Bible, of course, a coffee, but I was on mission, too busy to pause. But not Christie. She followed behind, picking up the pieces of my messy evangelism. She cupped frost-bitten hands, looked people in the eyes, encountered their stories.

She was gentle. Gentle, with God's children and their fears. She tucked them into the cleft of the rock and whispered God's Word to them.

"These voices speak of peace, kindness, gentleness ... and most of all, love," writes Henri Nouwen. "They might at first seem small and insignificant, and we may have a hard time trusting them. However, they are very persistent and they will grow stronger if we keep listening. . . . They are part of God's voice calling us from all eternity: 'My beloved child, my favorite one, my joy.'"[1]

In the following pages, you'll hear His voice calling you, friend, tenderly, into the cleft of a rock. People might say you're hiding, and you can say boldly, "Yes, I am. I'm safe in my Father's arms, like a stone in a sling." And then He'll use you, friend, like that stone, to conquer giants, but from a secret, hidden place, a tender place, a misunderstood place.

Ephesians 4:2 (NIV) says to be completely gentle. I've always been soft of tongue. I move carefully and people say I am gentle. I long to tread light, to bring light, to carry people into the quiet place. But God challenged me the other day saying there were parts of me I had not resigned to gentleness. There were "rights" I was still holding on to that were keeping me from being completely gentle. Like the "right" to get angry, or to defend myself. He showed me He wanted to remake those places, to make them gentle too, and this was surrender for me. How to be both angry and gentle? He would show me. Much as a sheath, He hides us, so we might be saved—and used for very special purposes. Gentleness protects, preserves, and carries power.

Enter in, friends. The Word awaits. God is with you.

—Emily T. Wierenga
Author, *God Who Became Bread*

---

1. Henri J. M. Nouwen, *Can You Drink the Cup?* (Notre Dame, IN: Ave Maria Press, 2006), 95.

INTRODUCTION

Christians are often considered, by the non-Christian world, to be a big part of the world's problems. Anyone can look around online and in person and see Christians who are causing more problems than they solve. But I know many Christians who are real, authentic, and changing their communities. These folks aren't the ones making the headlines. Instead, they are serving the poor, advocating for the vulnerable, caring for the lost, and drawing people toward Christ in a deep, countercultural way. What is the defining characteristic of most Christians who are making a deep impact, even if unnoticed by the world? Gentleness. In fact, Jonathan Edwards wrote that "a lamblike, dovelike spirit and temper" is "*the* true, and distinguishing disposition of the hearts of Christians"[2] while lamenting that he could definitely use more gentleness in his life.

Both Christian and secular culture consider gentleness to be a weakness, but it's actually the very opposite. Jesus is called the Lion of Judah and the Lamb of God, and somehow, the gentleness of the Lamb does not negate the power of the Lion. The more power someone has, the more radical gentleness becomes.

In a world of outrage and hate, where everyone chooses sides and camps and opinions, firing shots at anyone with an opposing view, we may think that Christians can't afford to look weak. But the

2. Dane Ortlund, "Want to Be Like Jesus? Be Gentle," *The Gospel Coalition*, October 17, 2018, www.thegospelcoalition.org/article/want-jesus-gentle.

Christian response is not to pick a side and fire more shots. It's found in the words of Christ, Paul, and many other biblical writers: laying down our lives, loving our enemies, and picking up our cross. Because of the radical gentleness of Christ, we are equipped to respond to our own enemies with gentleness. Sometimes those enemies are online, in our church (or other churches), or in our own family.

Proverbs 15:1 (NIV) says, *"A gentle answer turns away wrath,"* and this, right now, is what our world needs. Our world needs to know that Jesus was the *ultimate* gentle answer who turned away wrath and because of His sacrifice and the indwelling of the Holy Spirit, we also have the power to live out these words. We need to become gentle with our children, grandchildren, and husbands, we need to be gentle with our mothers and irritating uncles and that person who gets on our nerves, and we need to become gentle in the way we speak and lead.

When we become truly gentle, the world around us begins to change.

In his book, *A Gentle Answer,* Scott Sauls writes, "Only when we embody a bold gentleness will our outraged world begin to notice that we are distinctly his disciples. When we do this, and only when we do this, will an outraged world stop identifying Christians as a core part of the problem, and instead begin believing that Christians are a most necessary part of the solution."[3]

To do this, we need God. In an article for *The Gospel Coalition,* Dane Ortlund writes:

> The lofty theological discourse of Ephesians 1–3 funnels down, above all else, into an aroma of gentleness exuded by ordinary Christians in their ordinary lives. Yet such an aroma isn't ordinary. It's extraordinary, supernatural. It's where the Spirit takes us.[4]

3. Scott Sauls, *A Gentle Answer: Our "Secret Weapon" in an Age of Us Against Them* (Nashville, TN: Thomas Nelson, 2020), 184. Used by permission of HarperCollins Christian Publishing. www.harpercollinschristian.com.
4. Ortlund, "Want to Be Like Jesus? Be Gentle."

True gentleness is a work of the Holy Spirit inside us.

Together, we'll take the journey of gentleness. We'll discover what gentleness actually is (and what it's not) as well as how the Father, Son, and Holy Spirit all show true gentleness toward us. As Watchman Nee, a powerful Christian teacher from China, noted, "Often we try to be meek and gentle without knowing what it means to let God work in us the meekness and gentleness *of Christ*."[5] We're going to take an extra close look at the meekness and gentleness of Jesus. We'll discover how to actually grow in gentleness (since sitting on our hands or biting our lips until they bleed isn't working very well), as well as the radical way that Christ calls us to treat our enemies. I pray that this devotional will inspire and equip you, and that at the end, you'll look back and praise God for all He's done in you.

Growing with you,
Christie Thomas

Note: This devotional uses Million Praying Moms' "Think, Pray, Praise" method of daily prayer. If you are not familiar with this prayer practice, please visit: www.millionprayingmoms.com/the-think-pray-praise-method-of-daily-prayer.

---

5. Watchman Nee, *Sit, Walk, Stand: The Process of Christian Maturity* (Fort Washington, PA: CLC Publications, 2009), 36.

DAY 1

HOW TO HOLD A BABY

Let your gentleness be evident to all. The Lord is near.
—Philippians 4:5 (NIV)

When the nurses first laid my newborn son in my arms, I couldn't believe how tiny he was. From the itty-bitty wrinkled feet to the little cheeks that would soon fill out, he was small, red, and so very vulnerable. No one laid him in my arms and said to me, "I hope he's gentle with you!" Even though I was stapled and glued together after my C-section, it would have been ludicrous to consider a newborn baby to be gentle or ungentle. Despite my weakness after twenty-four hours of labor and an emergency surgery, I was the one who held the power in the situation. I needed to be gentle with my little son because I could easily hurt him. He was weak, so I needed to be gentle with him.

We often think of gentleness as weakness, but the two are very different. Someone who is weak doesn't need to be gentle; rather, it's the strong who need to practice gentleness. True gentleness is much more than being kind, tender, or mild-mannered. In fact, I consider gentleness to be the radical cousin of kindness because while anyone can be kind, a person can only truly be gentle when they have strength. Gentleness occurs when someone with power holds back for the sake of the vulnerable, as I did with my newborn son.

If you've thought of gentleness as a weakness in the past, you're in good company. Even the prophet Jonah thought of gentleness as weakness. After he preached to the people of Nineveh, they repented, and God decided not to cause the destruction He had planned. He held back His power for the sake of the vulnerable, and Jonah was livid. He railed at God, *"I knew that you are a gracious and compassionate God, slow to anger, abounding in faithful love, and one who relents from sending disaster. And now,* LORD, *take my life from me, for it is better for me to die than to live"* (Jonah 4:2–3). Jonah literally wanted to die because he was so frustrated over God's gentleness. (#dramaqueen.) Yes, this was the same God who had recently shown the same gentleness toward Jonah, but he now saw God's gentleness as a weakness, not as a strength.

Like Jonah, our world doesn't value gentleness. The world says we should seek power over others and grasp for control. It's not interested in holding back power for the sake of others. As Christians, we're often guilty of this too. We long to receive the grace of God's gentleness without having to extend that same gentleness to others. We see gentleness as a weakness so we choose to ignore that part of God's character.

But together over the next thirty days, we will uncover how gentleness is a sign of strength, something to pray for and practice, not to avoid. Because it's so countercultural, gentleness is one of the most obvious markers of a Christian who is growing in faith and godly character.

SOMETHING TO THINK ABOUT

When I first broached the topic of this devotional with some readers, one mentioned that the gentleness section in my book *Fruit Full*[6] had a huge impact on her. She said, "It challenged me to think of gentleness in a much broader and more applicable way, not just knowing how to pet a kitten." Gentleness is definitely much more than knowing how to pet a kitten or hold a baby. In fact, God's gentleness is the very crux of the gospel! Without Jesus's choice to hold back His power for the sake of humanity, He would never have gone to the cross for us.

6. Christie Thomas, *Fruit Full: 100 Family Experiences for Growing in the Fruit of the Spirit* (Grand Rapids, MI: Kregel Publications, 2022).

At this point, you may not be excited about growing in gentleness. If you've been steeped in a culture that sees gentleness as weakness, it may take a heart shift before you're ready to let God work in you in this way. But as Paul taught the Philippians, *"It is God who is working in you both to will and to work according to his good purpose"* (Philippians 2:13). When we invite Him to do His work in our hearts, God will give us a vision for Christlike gentleness and the desire to grow in it.

EXTRA VERSES FOR STUDY OR PRAYER

Jonah 4

VERSE OF THE DAY

Let your gentleness be evident to all. The Lord is near.

—Philippians 4:5 (NIV)

PRAYER

Lord, I confess that I've not always considered gentleness to be a virtue. In this world of grasping, one-upping, and outrage, gentleness seems like a great way to get walked all over. Please give me a vision for Christlike gentleness and the desire to grow in it. Remove my fear of seeming weak and help me to trust that true gentleness is life-changing. In Jesus's name, amen.

THINK

PRAY

PRAISE

TO-DO

PRAYER LIST

QUESTIONS FOR DEEPER REFLECTION

1. Think about a recent time when you or someone you know showed gentleness. Did it feel like strength or weakness in that moment?

2. How does the definition of gentleness as a sign of strength change the way you view that situation?

DAY 2

HE IS STRONG

Where were you when I established the earth?
Tell me, if you have understanding. Who fixed its dimensions?
Certainly you know! Who stretched a measuring line across it?
—Job 38:4–5

"*In the beginning God created the heavens and the earth*" (Genesis 1:1). You've probably heard this verse before, as it's the first line of the whole Bible. We can act blasé about it, but have you ever stopped to think about what this really means?

Our universe is so big, the closest star to our sun is 4.24 light years away, meaning its light takes 4.24 years to get to our eyes. In 2022, astronomers using the Hubble space telescope spotted a star that was 12.9 billion light years away.[7] That means the universe is so astronomically huge, even light takes billions of years to reach us. Every time I see pictures of galaxies and nebulas, I get a little queasy inside. Here I am on this little blue dot in this enormous universe, and God is so mighty, He created it all with His Word.

That's how much power God has. And yet when Adam and Eve ate the fruit of the Tree of Knowledge of Good and Evil, then hastily hid among the trees, God simply asked, "*Where are you?*" (Genesis 3:9). Adam and Eve had made themselves "*God's enemies*" (Romans 5:10 NIV). There were consequences to their actions, but even in that

7. NASA Hubble Mission Team, "Record Broken: Hubble Spots Farthest Star Ever Seen," March 30, 2022, science.nasa.gov/missions/hubble/record-broken-hubble-spots-farthest-star-ever-seen.

pivotal moment, God held back His power for the sake of the vulnerable. He clothed Adam and Eve, gave them a promise of a future Redeemer, and sent them away from the garden. This may seem harsh, but if they'd eaten from the Tree of Life after their disobedience, their curse would have been extended into eternity. Even the consequence was a protection, showing the gentleness of God.

The most creative minds on our planet can't fathom this kind of gentleness. My family recently watched a movie where a character with god-like powers tried to create a perfect race of people to inhabit his perfect world. When his creations failed him, did he simply say, "Where are you" like our God? Oh, no. This guy blew up the planet and went somewhere else to try again. He felt he had the right to this because he bred them, which is very different from God creating the universe out of nothing with a single word. Only the one true God has the right to blow up our planet and start again, but from the beginning, He chose to be gentle toward us. Even at His most frustrated, He saved a family to survive through the flood.

SOMETHING TO THINK ABOUT

In order to understand God's gentleness, we first need to appreciate His strength.

In Psalm 18, David describes God like one might describe a dragon the size of a skyscraper:

> *Then the earth shook and quaked; the foundations of the mountains trembled; they shook because he burned with anger. Smoke rose from his nostrils, and consuming fire came from his mouth; coals were set ablaze by it. He bent the heavens and came down, total darkness beneath his feet. He rode on a cherub and flew, soaring on the wings of the wind. He made darkness his hiding place, dark storm clouds his canopy around him. From the radiance of his presence, his clouds swept onward with hail and blazing coals. The Lord thundered from heaven; the Most High made his voice heard. He shot his arrows and scattered them; he hurled lightning bolts and routed them. The depths of the sea*

> *became visible, the foundations of the world were exposed, at your rebuke, Lord, at the blast of the breath of your nostrils.*
> —Psalm 18:7–15

Just a few verses later, David speaks of this same God clothing him and holding him securely on a mountain peak:

> *God—he clothes me with strength and makes my way perfect. He makes my feet like the feet of a deer and sets me securely on the heights.* —Psalm 18:32–33

Gentleness occurs when someone with great power holds back for the sake of someone weaker, and that's exactly what we see in these verses. David describes God as a being so powerful the mountains tremble, but also as the one who keeps the mountains from trembling so David can stand firm. This is the same God who fixed the dimensions of our world, and the same God who *"will protect your coming and going both now and forever"* (Psalm 121:8). As my favorite Sunday school song says, "We are weak but He is strong."

EXTRA VERSES FOR STUDY OR PRAYER

Job 38; Psalm 33; Psalm 89:1–18

VERSE OF THE DAY

Where were you when I established the earth? Tell me, if you have understanding. Who fixed its dimensions? Certainly you know! Who stretched a measuring line across it? —Job 38:4–5

PRAYER

I worship You, God, for You are more powerful than I could ever imagine. You made the earth with a word. You breathed and stars came into being. Help me never to lose sight of the power You hold because it's only in glimpsing Your power that I truly appreciate how much You hold back for my sake. In Jesus's name, amen.

THINK

PRAY

PRAISE

TO-DO

PRAYER LIST

QUESTIONS FOR DEEPER REFLECTION

1. Make a list of things in nature that make you say "wow."

2. Use this list to praise God for His power and might.

DAY 3

THE FATHER HEART OF GOD

It was I who taught Ephraim to walk, taking them by the hand,
but they never knew that I healed them.
—Hosea 11:3

Each of my sons began to walk when they were around a year old. The first clue that each would soon be ready to walk came when he began to pull himself up on every raised surface. The couch, a box on the floor, and legs (both mine and the chair's)—all were fair game to a little baby eager for his next steps. Soon, he'd be cruising along while holding the edge of the couch or gleefully pushing a box across the floor. The biggest challenge for me was weeks of leaning over at a back-breaking ninety-degree angle to steady his little hands as he took step after tentative step. But it was all worth it when he took his first few steps completely alone. His father and I laughed and cheered as each child learned to walk on his own.

My sons are now in the learn-to-drive stage rather than the learn-to-walk stage, but I still think of those precious (and taxing) moments when I read Hosea 11. In it, God compares His role in Israel's growth to that of a young father. He says:

> *It was I who taught Ephraim to walk, taking them by the hand, but they never knew that I healed them. I led them with human cords, with ropes of love. To them I was like one who eases the*

> *yoke from their jaws; I bent down to give them food.*
>
> —Hosea 11:3–4

This tender imagery reminds me of a father teaching his beloved child to walk, or a plowman caring for treasured oxen. The father has power over his young child and the plowman has control over his oxen, but both metaphors show God treating His people with gentle care. These images are followed by God's frustration at Israel's people for their refusal to repent. Like a wise father who can see the possible consequences of his young son's actions, God knows their sins will bring destruction. Although Israel is bent on turning from God, He will not turn from them.

> *I will not vent the full fury of my anger; I will not turn back to destroy Ephraim. For I am God and not man, the Holy One among you; I will not come in rage.* —Hosea 11:9

God is angry because their sin will lead to destructive consequences, but He chooses to hold back the full fury of His anger for the sake of His beloved children because He is God and holds Himself to a higher standard.

Despite Israel's consistent infidelity toward God, He refuses to obliterate them. Instead of raging at them, yelling, "I brought you into this world and I can take you back out of it," God laments what is about to happen to them. Later, He says that He will roar like a lion, using His voice to guide His children home from their time of bondage, settling them in their homes like a mother welcoming home a wayward child.

SOMETHING TO THINK ABOUT

In this passage, God's Father heart toward Israel is on full display: the tender memories of early childhood, the frustration with their current rebellion, and His future plans to draw them back home and settle them in safety.

God's relationship with Israel mirrors the one He has with you and me. God is the one who tenderly drew us toward His heart in the first place. Once we choose to place our trust in Him, the Creator of the universe curves His star-placing hand around ours, helping us take tentative steps into freedom and forgiveness. When we stray, He allows pertinent consequences instead of sending lightning to strike us dead, with the ultimate goal of drawing us back home, into His arms.

Whether you've had a good experience with a father figure or not, I pray that God would reveal His gentle heart of perfect fatherly love toward you today. May knowing how cherished you are help you take one more trusting step into God's way of gentleness.

EXTRA VERSES FOR STUDY OR PRAYER

Hosea 11:1–11

VERSE OF THE DAY

It was I who taught Ephraim to walk, taking them by the hand, but they never knew that I healed them. —Hosea 11:3

PRAYER

Lord, thank You for Your gentle heart of love toward Israel and toward me. Help me see You as a delighted father rather than as an angry dictator. Thank You for holding back Your right to vent the full fury of Your anger for my sake. Help me trust You to ease the yoke of slavery to sin from my jaw and give me food, the Bread of Life. In Jesus's name, amen.

THINK

PRAY

PRAISE

TO-DO

PRAYER LIST

QUESTIONS FOR DEEPER REFLECTION

1. How have you experienced fatherhood? How is it similar to or different from the way God describes Himself in our verse of the day?

2. Describe a time when you were bent on turning away from God. How did He draw you back?

DAY 4

GOD'S RESPONSE TO OUR SIN

A gentle answer turns away wrath.
—Proverbs 15:1 (NIV)

My stomach clenched as I checked my email for the umpteenth time that morning. I still hadn't received a response to the question I had asked, and I had a sudden, gut-churning realization that my husband and I had probably been scammed. Over the next few hours, I discovered my gut had been right. (Too bad it hadn't warned me earlier.) We had just welcomed our second baby and couldn't afford to lose that money, but it was gone forever into the pocket of a nameless con artist. We had been suckered in by someone whose full intent was to harm us by stealing our money. I wanted to call down God's wrath, but I had no idea who was behind the faceless email account.

I know a lot of people who are put off by talk of God's wrath. We don't like the thought of God being angry with us. After all, God is loving and kind, right? God *is* loving and kind, but He's also righteous and holy, which means He's perfectly set apart because of His moral perfection. God hates evil, and when I really think about it, I'm very glad He hates evil.

God is wrathful toward the kind of behaviors we should all find repulsive: abusing children and elderly people, destroying innocence, and taking advantage of the vulnerable. But Colossians 3:5–6 says God's wrath is also coming because of behaviors like *"sexual immorality, impurity, lust, evil desire, and greed, which is idolatry."* God is also against *"anger, wrath, malice, slander, and filthy language from your mouth"* (Colossians 3:8), in addition to lying, complaining, disobedience to parents, and many more behaviors that stem from a selfish and hard heart. I don't know about you, but I've definitely been guilty of many of those at some time or another in my life.

Because of our selfish hearts, we sin against each other in big and small ways every day, and this is the sin that breaks the world. Our selfishness breaks relationships by causing us to do things that hurt others—from the cruel words we speak to our kids in a moment of anger to jealous gossip in the workplace, from callous words written on social media to outright cheering for the annihilation of a people group.

SOMETHING TO THINK ABOUT

God has the right to condemn all of humanity, to pour out His wrath on all of us. None of us are immune to the selfishness that leads to sin. *"All have sinned and fall short of the glory of God"* (Romans 3:23). All of us—the scammer who stole my money, the world's worst dictators, and even our sweet children—have sinned and fallen short of God's perfection. But in His mercy and grace, God chose to hold back His full wrath and pour it out only on Himself. He chose to make Himself human, to live a sinless life, and to take the consequences for sin on Himself through death on the cross.

> *Once you were alienated and hostile in your minds as expressed in your evil actions. But now he has reconciled you by his physical body through his death, to present you holy, faultless, and blameless before him.* —Colossians 1:21–22

We did nothing to earn God's love or endear ourselves to God. In fact, the Bible says we were downright hostile to God! But God's answer to our sin isn't rightful punishment or eternal separation from Him. Instead, God's answer to our sin is gentleness. His sacrifice is the ultimate gentle answer that turns away wrath, holding back His power for our sake because He knew we wouldn't be able to survive His wrath. Jesus chose to submit Himself to the Father's wrath against sin on our behalf and was the only one who could turn an impossible situation into reconciliation between sinful humanity and God. Jesus is the ultimate gentle answer to turn away the justified wrath of God.

EXTRA VERSES FOR STUDY OR PRAYER

Romans 1:28–2:8; Romans 8:1–4

VERSE OF THE DAY

A gentle answer turns away wrath. —Proverbs 15:1 (NIV)

PRAYER

Lord, thank You for giving a gentle answer to Your own wrath, turning it away from us and toward Yourself. I was alienated from You, but You reconciled me by Your own body, through death, so that I could stand holy, faultless, and blameless before You. I am so grateful for Your gentleness toward me. Help me to live in this reality and share Your gentleness with those around me. In Jesus's name, amen.

THINK

PRAY

PRAISE

TO-DO

PRAYER LIST

QUESTIONS FOR DEEPER REFLECTION

1. Prayerfully read Romans 1:28–32. Which have you personally lived out? Confess these to God, allowing Him to reconcile you.

2. Imagine you are standing before God. How does He now see you? (Not sure? Read Colossians 1:22.) Write down any thoughts and feelings that rise up in response.

DAY 5

GOD'S RESPONSE TO OUR WEAKNESS

Then the angel of the Lord returned for a second time and touched him. He said, "Get up and eat, or the journey will be too much for you."
—1 Kings 19:7

The Hebrew version of the name Elijah literally means "Yahweh is my God," which makes a lot of sense when you look at the life of Elijah the prophet. God called Elijah to ministry during a time when the rulers of Israel were leading the entire country into evil and idolatry. I doubt being an Israelite prophet was ever fun, but this time period must have been one of the most dangerous. The queen was slaughtering Yahweh's prophets like they were flies at a picnic, and the king spent more time moping about vineyards he coveted than leading his people well.

In a moment of godly courage, Elijah, the only prophet who wasn't in hiding, met King Ahab and his four hundred and fifty false priests at the top of Mount Carmel. (See 1 Kings 18.) What followed was an epic display of God's power over the utter impotence of the false god, Baal. The false priests couldn't get a single bit of flame to burn their sacrifice no matter how they danced and cut themselves in frantic worship.

After hours of this, Elijah calmly dumped twelve pots of water on the Lord's altar and offering (not an easy feat after three years of drought). Then he simply prayed. No dancing, no cutting, no theatrics aside from the precious water being dumped. Immediately, fire fell from heaven, burning up the sacrifice, the altar, and all the water. Now *that's* true power, and the people of Israel knew it. They turned back to Yahweh en masse. Afterward, God lifted the drought by finally sending rain on His repentant people.

You'd think after all this, Elijah would be humming with excitement, thrilled at the power of God and delighted to watch what would happen next. Instead, he received a death threat from the queen and ran for his life. There, in the wilderness, he collapsed under a broom tree and prayed for death. Elijah was done. Worn out. Utterly exhausted and ready for it all to be over.

God knew Elijah didn't need another reminder of His incredible power at the moment. Instead, in a gesture of utmost gentleness, God sent an angel to feed Elijah.

When Elijah woke, he found a hot loaf of bread and a jug of water next to his head. He ate, drank, and fell back asleep. *"Then the angel of the LORD returned for a second time and touched him. He said, 'Get up and eat, or the journey will be too much for you.' So he got up, ate, and drank"* (1 Kings 19:7–8).

Later, Elijah trekked forty days and nights to the mountain where, long ago, God revealed Himself to the fresh-from-slavery Hebrews. In that moment, the mountain had been *"completely enveloped in smoke because the LORD came down on it in fire. Its smoke went up like the smoke of a furnace, and the whole mountain shook violently"* (Exodus 19:18). God put on such a display of power that anyone who touched the mountain would die.

I wonder if Elijah expected the same show of power again on the mountaintop. After all, he knew God could do it; he had witnessed God's terrifying power on Mount Carmel. So he stood on the mountain, waiting for the Lord's presence. Only this time, God knew Elijah didn't need smoke, fire, or earthquakes. Instead, God spoke through a soft whisper. Elijah recognized God in the whisper and poured out his frustration and pain to God.

SOMETHING TO THINK ABOUT

God could have lambasted Elijah for his sudden lack of faith, but instead, He chose to hold back His power for the sake of the worn-out, vulnerable prophet. God chose to feed Elijah and let him take a nap, then He chose to reveal Himself through a whisper on the wind. This wasn't a sign of weakness on God's part, but a sign of strength, power, and tender love.

Are you in a place of weariness or burnout today? God is not surprised. Just as He knew what Elijah needed, He knows what you need. Just as Elijah poured out his frustration to God and received real solutions in response, you can do the same, trusting that God will help you. Are you ready to receive His gentleness?

EXTRA VERSES FOR STUDY OR PRAYER

First Kings 18–19

VERSE OF THE DAY

Then the angel of the L*ORD* *returned for a second time and touched him. He said, "Get up and eat, or the journey will be too much for you."* —1 Kings 19:7

PRAYER

Lord, thank You for Your gentleness toward me. You could reveal Yourself only in Your immense power, but You know that's not always what I need. Thank You for knowing what I need and for providing it. Help me to trust You for my daily bread, for wisdom to solve the problems I encounter, and for the strength to continue. In Jesus's name, amen.

THINK

PRAY

PRAISE

TO-DO

PRAYER LIST

QUESTIONS FOR DEEPER REFLECTION

1. Describe a time you felt exhausted, overwhelmed, or worn out from life.

2. With a spirit ready to hear from God, ask Him, "Where were You in that moment?" Write down what comes to mind.

DAY 6

THE GOOD SHEPHERD

I am the good shepherd.
The good shepherd lays down his life for the sheep.
—John 10:11

I squirmed in my uncomfortable chair in the lecture theater, stomach twisting in knots. I had never asked a question in front of a large group before, but in this introductory class to the New Testament, I dug up enough courage to ask one I'd been wrestling with for months. The professor called on me. With sweaty hands and a pounding heart, I asked, "Why did Jesus keep telling those He healed to stay quiet about their miracle when He knew they'd just go tell everyone anyway? Wasn't He forcing them to sin?"

I can't remember exactly what my professor said that day, but I have an answer now. Jesus told them not to talk about their healings because He wasn't ready to reveal Himself as Messiah yet. In fact, Jesus actively *"gave the disciples orders to tell no one that he was the Messiah"* (Matthew 16:20). Here's why He didn't want anyone to know: the word *Messiah* was steeped in centuries of expectations of violence. Everyone who had previously proclaimed himself *Messiah* or *King of Israel* took his power through bloodshed and force. Jesus had to redefine the word *Messiah* before He could let it fully label Him.

To do this, Jesus embarked on a mission of reeducation. When His imprisoned cousin sent messengers to ask if He really was the Messiah, Jesus didn't wave a sword around, lop off the head of a

Roman, and shout, "Now do you believe Me?" Instead, He told the messengers, *"Go and report to John what you hear and see: the blind receive their sight, the lame walk, those with leprosy are cleansed, the deaf hear, the dead are raised, and the poor are told the good news"* (Matthew 11:4–5). This is what God's kingdom actually looks like: power harnessed for good instead of violence.

During His reeducation campaign, Jesus referred to Himself as the Good Shepherd. As the Good Shepherd, Jesus *"protects his flock like a shepherd; he gathers the lambs in his arms and carries them in the fold of His garment. He gently leads those that are nursing"* (Isaiah 40:11). These verses don't refer to a weak shepherd, but a strong one who *"comes with strength"* and whose *"power establishes his rule"* (Isaiah 40:10). There is nothing weak about our Good Shepherd, but He is so, so gentle toward us. Jesus has the authority to lay down His life for His sheep and *"the right to take it up again"* (John 10:18). He chooses to use that authority to gather us, His wayward lambs, in His arms.

Jesus was so insistent on the way of gentleness and humility that Peter began to get uncomfortable with all His talk of dying. One day, frustrated with Jesus's predictions of death, he pulled Jesus into a private conversation and said, *"Oh no, Lord! This will never happen to you!"* (Matthew 16:22). Jesus didn't turn to him and say, "You know what? You're right. I need to just fight My way to the top. Why didn't I think of that earlier?" Rather, *"Jesus turned and told Peter, 'Get behind me, Satan! You are a hindrance to me because you're not thinking about God's concerns but human concerns'"* (Matthew 16:23). That is a mighty stern rebuke! If I had been in Peter's place, I probably would have burst into tears.

SOMETHING TO THINK ABOUT

Gentleness can sometimes feel a bit ambiguous. What does it even look like in real life? While we can look to amazing people of faith like Corrie ten Boom or Mother Teresa, we also have an epic example in Jesus, who turned *Messiah* from a word coated in centuries of blood into a word that displays the Shepherd-heart of God. To know what gentleness looks like, we should start with Jesus, our Good Shepherd, who laid down His life instead of fighting for power and then picked it back up again so we could have life to the full.

EXTRA VERSES FOR STUDY OR PRAYER

Isaiah 40

VERSE OF THE DAY

I am the good shepherd. The good shepherd lays down his life for the sheep. —John 10:11

PRAYER

Jesus, You are the Good Shepherd and I am Your sheep. Thank You for choosing the path of gentleness toward sinners, choosing to lay down Your life for us and take it back up again so we might truly live. Help me to see the gospel through fresh eyes so I can see what gentleness looks like in real life. In Jesus's name, amen.

THINK

PRAY

PRAISE

TO-DO

PRAYER LIST

QUESTIONS FOR DEEPER REFLECTION

1. As you read Isaiah 40, circle the words that point to God's strength and underline words that point to God's gentleness. Talk to God about what you uncover.

2. Ask Jesus how He wants to show Himself as a Good Shepherd to you today. Write down what comes to mind.

DAY 7

THE LION AND THE LAMB

Then one of the elders said to me,
"Do not weep. Look, the Lion from the tribe of Judah,
the Root of David, has conquered so that he is able to open the
scroll and its seven seals."
—Revelation 5:5

As a Navy SEAL, Steve trained in and utilized hand-to-hand combat and marksmanship during his active missions. Steve was a trained killer, like a lion who knew exactly when and how to catch his prey and take it down as quickly as possible. But then the lion with blood on his hands met the Lamb who was slain, and his life was forever changed. He turned from a life of violence and became a Navy chaplain. This choice displayed more strength than any other choice he'd made before. Only someone with true strength can choose to be gentle, which is exactly what Steve did.[8]

Jesus wasn't a trained sniper but He is even more powerful:

> *He is the image of the invisible God, the firstborn over all creation. For everything was created by him, in heaven and on earth, the visible and the invisible, whether thrones or dominions or rulers or authorities—all things have been created through him and for him. He is before all things, and by him all things hold together.* —Colossians 1:15–17

8. Steve's story is told in his book: Steve Watkins, *Meeting God Behind Enemy Lines: A Christian Testimony as a US Navy SEAL* (The Woodlands, TX: Kress Christian Publications, 1999).

There is not a bone in Jesus's body, not a neuron in His brain, not a cell in His liver that is *not* the image of the invisible God, holding all things in the entire universe together. Revelation 5:5 calls Jesus the conquering Lion of Judah, and there has never been a moment in all of history when Jesus didn't have the power to blast His enemies or turn our planet to dust and start again.

But the Lion of Judah chose not to use His unimaginable power for Himself. Instead, He *"did not consider equality with God as something to be exploited. Instead he emptied himself by assuming the form of a servant, taking on the likeness of humanity. And when he had come as a man, he humbled himself by becoming obedient to the point of death—even to death on a cross"* (Philippians 2:6–8).

The Lion of Judah chose to become the Lamb who was slain, laying down His life so He could ransom us from sin and death and bring us into His kingdom. The only way He could do this was to lay down His power for the sake of the vulnerable, and in the laying down of His power, allow Himself to be murdered. Gentleness doesn't come any more spectacularly than that.

SOMETHING TO THINK ABOUT

Jesus is both 100 percent Lion and 100 percent Lamb, holding immense power but allowing His own death because He knew His death and resurrection was the only way to have a true relationship with us.

I'm reminded of one of Jesus's toughest teachings: *"But I tell you, don't resist an evildoer. On the contrary, if anyone slaps you on your right cheek, turn the other to him also"* (Matthew 5:39). It seems like weakness to turn the other cheek, but a weak person would more likely crumple into a ball and cry in the corner. A powerful person would slap back extra hard. Only the person with enormous power and unshakable self-confidence will be able to stand tall, refuse to take revenge, and turn the other cheek. That's the way of Christlike gentleness.

In every situation, we have the choice to react out of weakness, power, or Christlike gentleness, and gentleness is the hardest of the three. But as Scott Sauls points out, "We must become settled in the truth that whatever Jesus asks from us, He has already done for us."[9] Jesus, our Lion and Lamb, has gone first into the radical way of gentleness, and He calls us forward into this way of life. When faced with opposition this week and tempted to react like a lion, let's take a moment to pray, harness that power, and use it to represent Christ well. Knowing that we are His beloved children, there is no need for us to take up the defense. We can show the same strong gentleness to our family members, our coworkers, and even our enemies.

EXTRA VERSES FOR STUDY OR PRAYER

Matthew 21:5; Philippians 2:5–11; Revelation 5

VERSE OF THE DAY

Then one of the elders said to me, "Do not weep. Look, the Lion from the tribe of Judah, the Root of David, has conquered so that he is able to open the scroll and its seven seals."

—Revelation 5:5

PRAYER

Jesus, I praise You because You are both the undefeatable Lion of Judah and the Lamb who was slain. Open my eyes to how gentleness can be a show of great power and give me the ability to trust You in those moments when You call me to turn the other cheek. Thank You for going first in this way of gentleness and teach me to be more like You. In Jesus's name, amen.

THINK

9. Sauls, *A Gentle Answer*, 183–184.

PRAY

PRAISE

TO-DO

PRAYER LIST

QUESTIONS FOR DEEPER REFLECTION

1. In Philippians 2:5, Paul exhorts us to *"adopt the same attitude as that of Christ Jesus."* What kind of attitude was that? How does your attitude compare to Jesus's?

2. Philippians 2:10–11 gives a powerful image of everyone *"in heaven and on earth and under the earth"* bowing down and confessing that Jesus is Lord. Where do you imagine yourself in that crowd? Consider physically bowing down in front of Jesus right now.

DAY 8

MASTER OF ANGELS

Or do you think that I cannot call on my Father, and he will provide me here and now with more than twelve legions of angels?
—Matthew 26:53

If you had an angel army at your disposal, what would you do with it? Would you command the army to personally escort your vehicle to work each day? Or perhaps to keep your children from all kinds of harm? Or maybe to save you a spot in line at Costco?

In Matthew 26:53, Jesus said He had immediate access to at least twelve legions of angels. If you've ever wondered exactly how many angels that is, each Roman legion had four to six thousand soldiers, so Jesus was referring to an army of at least forty-eight thousand angels. That's an immense amount of power. And yet Jesus chose not to use this army in His time of need.

Imagine that you were there in the garden of Gethsemane with Jesus and His disciples. Stars peeked out from behind olive leaves and a nighttime animal snuffled nearby. Your big dinner made you drowsy and you struggled to keep your eyes open. Then you heard a rhythmic clanking coming from the other end of the garden. You jolted awake because you grew up to the sounds of marching soldiers and you know it bodes ill. The clanking got louder and torches bobbed through the night until a crowd surrounded you and your friends. It was a face-off: Jesus and His team versus the Pharisees and their team. (Except for your friend Judas, who, very strangely, appeared to be on the wrong team.)

> *Then Jesus, knowing everything that was about to happen to him, went out and said to them, "Who is it that you're seeking?" "Jesus of Nazareth," they answered. "I am he," Jesus told them. Judas, who betrayed him, was also standing with them. When Jesus told them, "I am he," they stepped back and fell to the ground.*
>
> —John 18:4–6

Jesus displayed His power in a single phrase, echoing the name the one true God gave Himself in Exodus 3:14: "*I AM WHO I AM.*" And what impact did that name have on the listeners? They stumbled backward and fell down. I've never introduced myself and had someone fall over at the sound of my name. It just doesn't have that kind of power. But Jesus's name and His truthful identification with the eternal God was enough to knock over the soldiers. They had to pick themselves up off the ground.

> *Then he asked them again, "Who is it that you're seeking?" "Jesus of Nazareth," they said. "I told you I am he," Jesus replied. "So if you're looking for me, let these men go." This was to fulfill the words he had said: "I have not lost one of those you have given me." Then Simon Peter, who had a sword, drew it, struck the high priest's servant, and cut off his right ear. (The servant's name was Malchus.)* —John 18:7–10

At every point in this true story, Jesus had the choice to end it all by calling down His angel army or continue to lay down His power for the sake of humanity. I think you know what He chose:

> *Then Jesus told him, "Put your sword back in its place because all who take up the sword will perish by the sword. Or do you think that I cannot call on my Father, and he will provide me here and now with more than twelve legions of angels? How, then, would the Scriptures be fulfilled that say it must happen this way?"*
>
> —Matthew 26:52–54

SOMETHING TO THINK ABOUT

The great I AM chose to withhold His power so the Scriptures could be fulfilled. Jesus knew Isaiah had predicted that He would be despised, rejected, and led like a lamb to the slaughter, not because He needed to be humiliated but because of God's promise:

> *He was pierced because of our rebellion, crushed because of our iniquities; punishment for our peace was on him, and we are healed by his wounds.* —Isaiah 53:5

With this goal in mind, Jesus could move forward in gentleness even in a time of great personal vulnerability, choosing to lay down His immense power in order to bring healing and reconciliation. As followers of Christ, we have the Holy Spirit inside of us and the power of Christ at our disposal. Knowing that the power of heaven is backing us up, we can choose to work for reconciliation without fear. If Christ is for us, who can stand against us?

EXTRA VERSES FOR STUDY OR PRAYER

Isaiah 53

VERSE OF THE DAY

> *Or do you think that I cannot call on my Father, and he will provide me here and now with more than twelve legions of angels?*
> —Matthew 26:53

PRAYER

Jesus, thank You for choosing to lay down Your right to defend Yourself so that we could be healed and brought into a right relationship with You. You had the ability to call down legions of angels, but You didn't do so in order that the Scriptures could be fulfilled. Thank You for valuing us that much. In Jesus's name, amen.

THINK

PRAY

PRAISE

TO-DO

PRAYER LIST

QUESTIONS FOR DEEPER REFLECTION

1. Jesus held back His power during a time of vulnerability. Do you think this is always true for how He expects His followers to behave? Why or why not?

2. Jesus was able to hold back His power because He knew His mission. How might knowing your mission help you hold back your own power in gentleness?

____

____

____

DAY 9

GENTLE AND LOWLY IN HEART

Take my yoke upon you, and learn from me, for I am gentle and lowly in heart, and you will find rest for your souls.
—Matthew 11:29 (ESV)

"Hey, Buddy, come here for a sec," I called from my spot on the couch. "What do you think gentleness means?"

My son looked at me quizzically, then patted me gently on the arm. "Like this," he said, then grunted and pushed hard on my arm. "Not like this." I winced.

"You mean gentleness is when you hold back your strength so you don't hurt someone?" He grinned and wandered away, satisfied that he had answered my question adequately, even though I'd provided the words.

Usually, our basic understanding of gentle people is similar to my son's. They are quiet and soft, not rough. They don't assert themselves. Maybe gentle people even seem like cowardly doormats, letting themselves get walked over by everyone. However, Jesus identifies His deepest self as *"gentle and lowly in heart,"* and a cursory look through the Gospels shows that He didn't fit our basic human understanding of gentleness. He wasn't quiet and soft with the Pharisees, He asserted Himself every time He spoke about the kingdom of God, and while He did let Himself be crucified, it wasn't because He was a cowardly doormat.

In various Bible translations of Matthew 11:29, the words *gentle* and *lowly* are interchangeable with *meek* and *humble*. All of these English words are translations of the single Greek word, *práos*, which "denotes the quality of gentle strength that rests in God's sovereignty. It is the settled disposition of spirit that refuses retaliation, surrenders personal rights to the Lord's will, and channels power through mercy."[10] Gentleness is starting to sound a lot more like humility than like "the opposite of rough," isn't it?

Rather than being the personality trait of someone quiet and submissive, gentleness is a character trait of people who trust God so much that they don't focus on themselves or their own needs. The Bible rarely contrasts gentleness with physical roughness. Instead, gentleness is contrasted with *"bitter envy and selfish ambition"* in James 3:13–14 and described as the opposite of being quarrelsome in 2 Timothy 2:24–25. Therefore, when Jesus calls Himself gentle and lowly, He means He:

- Fully trusts God's goodness and control in every situation
- Is not occupied with Himself
- Is not quarrelsome
- Is not jealous
- Does not have selfish ambitions

SOMETHING TO THINK ABOUT

Jesus was able to live a life of humility and gentleness because He fully trusted that His Father had His best interests at heart, and He knew His Father's goodness and control over the situation intimately. When we know we can deeply trust that God is good, loves us, and is in control in our lives, we'll also be able to live the kind of life that's not preoccupied with self. We'll be more than just "not rough" with our kids, our coworkers, and the people we meet on the Internet, but we'll choose to focus on the needs of others instead of our own needs and wants.

10. G4235. práos. *Strong's Greek Concordance*, biblehub.com/greek/4235.htm.

When we truly trust God to care for us, we won't be jealous because we'll know that God has our best interests in mind. We won't be quarrelsome because we won't constantly be trying to be right. We'll even be able to live out Paul's vision outlined in Philippians 2:3–4: *"Do nothing out of selfish ambition or conceit, but in humility consider others as more important than yourselves. Everyone should look not to his own interests, but rather to the interests of others."*

The only way we can live like this is when, like Jesus, we're so confident in God's goodness and power that we know we don't need to obsess about our own interests because God's got them in hand. We can hold back our own strength because we trust in God's strength on our behalf.

EXTRA VERSES FOR STUDY OR PRAYER

Philippians 2:1–4; 2 Timothy 2:24–25; James 3:13–14

VERSE OF THE DAY

Take my yoke upon you, and learn from me, for I am gentle and lowly in heart, and you will find rest for your souls.

—Matthew 11:29 (ESV)

PRAYER

Jesus, I praise You because You are gentle and lowly, not obsessing about Yourself or what's best for You, but considering our interests as even more important than Yours. I confess I don't usually live like this and often don't even *want* to live like this. Please change my heart and help me to trust in Your goodness and control over every situation. In Your name, amen.

THINK

PRAY

PRAISE

TO-DO

PRAYER LIST

QUESTIONS FOR DEEPER REFLECTION

1. The best way to learn to trust in God's goodness and control in every situation is to practice seeing Him at work in your past. Think of a situation in your life that felt out of your control. Looking back, can you see God's hand in it?

2. Describe a possible situation where fully trusting in God's goodness and control impacts the way you treat someone.

DAY 10

THE GENTLE PARTNER

Come to me, all of you who are weary and burdened, and I will give you rest. Take my yoke upon you and learn from me, because I am lowly and humble in heart, and you will find rest for your souls. For my yoke is easy and my burden is light.
—Matthew 11:28–30

"It doesn't make any sense," my son wailed. I tried not to sigh as I wiped my soapy hands off on a towel.

"Show me what you're working on," I requested. Still grumbling, he plopped down in front of the computer chair. I knew his math curriculum was hard but doable, and I also knew he would continue to struggle unless I sat beside him, actively encouraging him to persevere. Which is exactly what I did.

Together, we read through math problems and I half coached, half motivated him to work his way to the answers. It wasn't fast, but his attitude remarkably improved as I sat with him. He felt seen, heard, and helped.

This is exactly the image Jesus gave us in Matthew 11:28–30. When I was younger, I imagined this scene with God as a farmer and me as a trusty ox, plodding along with His light yoke around my neck. A yoke is a wooden frame farmers put on the necks of animals so they can pull a plow or wagon. When doing research for this verse for another project, I stumbled across a startling fact: oxen were yoked in pairs. (Obviously, I did not grow up on a farm.)

In this metaphor, Jesus isn't in the position of a farmer, beckoning me toward Him while He holds a yoke to lay across my back, prepping me to pull a plow (aka "do grand works for the kingdom of God"). He doesn't load me down with expectations. Rather, Jesus is in the position of an older, more practiced ox, patiently waiting for me to slip in beside Him, willingly joining Him in His work. As the older and more practiced ox, He walks beside me, carrying the burden of the yoke and the load, teaching me to trust His leading.

This means Jesus doesn't threaten us, saying, "Be gentler or else!" or "I'm sick of your selfishness! Time for punishment." As I wrote in my book *Fruit Full*:

> Instead, Jesus picks up your yoke of sin. (That yoke, by the way, was created by humans, not by Jesus.) He puts your yoke on His own back and invites you to walk with Him. Jesus does the heavy lifting while showing you how to live more like Him. His yoke is easy and His burden is light because He's doing most of the work. ... Your work is to give Jesus your yoke and let Him help you carry it.[11]

SOMETHING TO THINK ABOUT

What burdens are you carrying today? When we're trying to carry them all by ourselves, we can't possibly be gentle with anyone else because we're too busy being weary and burdened with the stuff we are supposed to let Jesus carry. When I'm weary and burdened, I don't have the bandwidth to sit with my son while he does his math. When I'm weary and burdened, I don't have a great filter, so I may speak harsh words to my husband instead of words tempered with wisdom and patience. When I'm weary and burdened, even a dog nudging my arm for a scratch can cause me to lose my cool. And I cause all this extra suffering in my world because I choose not to let Jesus help me carry my burdens.

11. Thomas, *Fruit Full*, 223.

Instead of trying to do the impossible on our own, let's practice sliding into that yoke beside Jesus. He'll give us a nod and a smile, speaking words of life while doing the heavy lifting, and we'll notice our ability to be gentle improve as we feel seen, heard, and helped.

EXTRA VERSES FOR STUDY OR PRAYER

Isaiah 42:1–4

VERSE OF THE DAY

Come to me, all of you who are weary and burdened, and I will give you rest. Take my yoke upon you and learn from me, because I am lowly and humble in heart, and you will find rest for your souls. For my yoke is easy and my burden is light.

—Matthew 11:28–30

PRAYER

Jesus, forgive me for trying to carry all my burdens on my own, instead of letting You help me. I give You the burden of my sin and the other things that weigh me down and I choose to let You help me with these burdens. Thank You for being my Helper and for Your easy and light burden. In Jesus's name, amen.

THINK

PRAY

PRAISE

TO-DO

PRAYER LIST

QUESTIONS FOR DEEPER REFLECTION

1. List the sins, situations, or attitudes that are leaving you weary and burdened today.

2. Consider why you haven't given them over before. Have you tried, but keep snatching them back? Have you simply forgotten? Or have you assumed you're better at carrying them than Jesus is?

DAY 11

ALIVE WITH GENTLENESS

But God, who is rich in mercy, because of his great love that he had for us, made us alive with Christ even though we were dead in trespasses. You are saved by grace!
—Ephesians 2:4–5

My friends and I swapped stories of times we'd been ungentle with our kids, and one mom compared her experience to vomiting. The anger and frustration had built up inside of her to the point where it spewed out, burning and angry, from her mouth. As it usually goes, she said more than she intended to say. And just like vomiting, she felt better afterward ... until she looked around and saw the mess she'd made.

Before and after the verbal vomit, she hadn't wanted to hurt her kids. But while she was spewing frustration, she did. She's not alone. Nearly every mom I know, including me, has a secret story of shamefully yelling at her small children at least once.

In Romans 7:15, Paul laments the same problem: *"For I do not understand what I am doing, because I do not practice what I want to do, but I do what I hate."* That's the sin inside us, the same sin that tempts moms to yell at their kids and all of the other harsh behaviors we are chagrined to find ourselves doing.

Thankfully, Paul also gives us the freeing truth about sin: *"Therefore, there is now no condemnation for those in Christ Jesus, because the law of the Spirit of life in Christ Jesus has set you free from the law of sin and death"* (Romans 8:1–2). We've been set free! And not only did God set us free from the law of sin and death through Jesus, *"He also raised us up with him and seated us with him in the heavens in Christ Jesus, so that in the coming ages he might display the immeasurable riches of his grace through his kindness to us in Christ Jesus"* (Ephesians 2:6–7). You and I are seated with Christ in the heavens! It is already done.

So why do we still struggle with sin? Why do we still do what we don't want to do? Why is gentleness so hard?

Watchman Nee said it's because "you are trying to walk before you have sat down, and in that way lies sure defeat … The secret of deliverance from sin is not to *do* something, but to rest on what God has done."[12] To put it simply, we're trying too hard. Instead of putting the full weight of our sin on Jesus like we put our full weight on a chair when we sit, we try to fix some of it ourselves. Rather than resting in Christ's finished work for us and letting His Spirit work to set us free from ungentleness, we keep struggling. Paul has very strong words for those who rely on rules and their own strength for their spiritual growth: *"Are you so foolish? After beginning by the Spirit, are you now finishing by the flesh?"* (Galatians 3:3).

As Watchman Nee so powerfully described it, "Christianity begins not with a big DO, but with a big DONE."[13] But sometimes, just like the Galatians, we can start our Christian life off by trusting in forgiveness through faith, yet continue to strive and try too hard. As Nee said, we forget that "from this point onward Christian experience proceeds as it began, not on the basis of our own work, but always on that of the finished work of Another."[14]

SOMETHING TO THINK ABOUT

How can we give those shameful moments when we've reacted in harshness to God and move forward in freedom? It starts with truly trusting that God is a joyful giver, that He wants to lavish His grace

12. Nee, *Sit, Walk, Stand*, 22.
13. Ibid, 14.
14. Ibid, 18.

on us. God's Spirit is given freely and fully, like a river of life, not in drips like a malfunctioning water fountain.

Consider the parable of the prodigal son. (See Luke 15:11–32.) When the son came home after squandering his father's wealth, he wasn't met with recriminations like, "Why didn't you try harder?" or "Now you have to work off your debt." Instead, the father gave him *more*. He gave the son a ring, a robe, and a party. The son came home and the Father gave him rest. Like the son, when you come to God, your Father will give you rest.

EXTRA VERSES FOR STUDY OR PRAYER

Romans 6:2–4; Galatians 2:20–21; Ephesians 1:13

VERSE OF THE DAY

But God, who is rich in mercy, because of his great love that he had for us, made us alive with Christ even though we were dead in trespasses. You are saved by grace! —Ephesians 2:4–5

PRAYER

God, You are rich in mercy and have made me alive with Christ because of Your great love, not because of anything I've done. In fact, I was dead in my trespasses! Thank You for saving me through grace and continuing to work in my life through Your Spirit. Help me to truly rest in You, to stop trying to be a better person on my own and believe that You have already seated me with Christ in the heavenly realms. May my identity in Christ shape me into the gentle person You've created me to be. In Jesus's name, amen.

THINK

PRAY

PRAISE

TO-DO

PRAYER LIST

QUESTIONS FOR DEEPER REFLECTION

1. What is a recent situation in which you tried to draw on your own strength instead of relying on God? How can you choose to rest in God's finished work today?

2. In Ephesians 2:6, we're not told to sit down but rather that we're already sitting in the heavens with Jesus. How could this understanding of your current position change the way you react to others?

DAY 12

FRUITFUL GENTLENESS

But the fruit of the Spirit is love, joy, peace, patience, kindness, goodness, faithfulness, gentleness, and self-control. The law is not against such things.
—Galatians 5:22–23

My son sprawled in my lap while I chatted with a friend. "I just learned how to be bold. How can I be quiet and gentle?" she asked. You may have said something very similar to yourself as we've walked through the concepts of God's gentleness toward us. As Christian women, we are often told to be more submissive, meeker, and gentler. Those aren't inherently bad personality traits, but they can be twisted to force women to be smaller and quieter than God intended us to be. If you've been told all your life that you are too much, too bold, or too loud, or if you, like my friend, have finally learned how to assert yourself, you may balk at the idea of becoming more gentle. It may feel like one more way to push women to be and act a certain way.

But here's the thing about gentleness: it's included in the apostle Paul's list of the fruit of the Spirit. He wouldn't have included gentleness as a fruit of Spirit-reliant living if only certain personality traits could live in gentleness. Gentleness can be exhibited by every Christian with every different personality, from the gruff gym teacher and eloquent lawyer to the soft-spoken preschool teacher and the ninety-year-old grandma.

Since we're talking about fruit, let's have a simple botany lesson on growth. If I have a peach tree in my backyard, I can't wave my finger at it and say, "Okay, Peachie, here's the deal. You're going to double your output of fruit this year. You're going to give it 100 percent, trying as hard as you can." Doesn't that sound ridiculous? If I really want to double my output of fruit, I have to consider the soil, including acidity levels, whether there's a lot of clay or rocks, and how many nutrients are likely still in it. I need to find the right fertilizer, make sure there isn't a nearby maple tree shading it out, and ensure it gets enough water. It needs food, water, air, sun, and soil to become fruitful.

If we want to grow the fruit of the Spirit in our lives, we have to do the same thing. I can't say to myself, "Okay, Christie, here's the deal. You're going to double your output of love, joy, peace, and gentleness this year. You're going to give it 100 percent, trying as hard as you can." Fruit doesn't come from a try-hard faith. Rather, if I want to grow in the Spirit's good fruit, I have to consider where my spiritual roots are. I need Jesus, who is my Bread of Life, living water, and the Light of the World. I need to be rooted and established in God's love; otherwise, the next big storm in life is going to topple me over.

SOMETHING TO THINK ABOUT

Gentleness doesn't mean being a quiet woman who never shares her opinions, never rocks the boat, and is never assertive. Rather, *"those who belong to Christ Jesus have crucified the flesh with its passions and desires"* (Galatians 5:24). Gentleness is about crucifying my ungodly passions, not changing my God-given personality. Jesus had moments of frustration and tears and passion, but He also displayed gentleness in His life. John, one of those who literally walked with Jesus for three years, wrote, *"The one who says he remains in him should walk just as he walked"* (1 John 2:6). You and I can't literally walk beside a physical Jesus, but when He went to heaven, He gave us the amazing gift of His Spirit. The only way to walk as Jesus walked is to live by the Spirit, keeping in step with Him daily. (See Galatians 5:25.) Trusting in the Spirit to help you is the only way to true, Christlike gentleness emanating from your soul, no matter what kind of personality you have.

EXTRA VERSES FOR STUDY OR PRAYER

Romans 8:9–10; Galatians 5:16–24; 1 Peter 3:3–4

VERSE OF THE DAY

But the fruit of the Spirit is love, joy, peace, patience, kindness, goodness, faithfulness, gentleness, and self-control. The law is not against such things. —Galatians 5:22–23

PRAYER

Jesus, I'm sorry for the times I've used my personality as an excuse not to be gentle. Thank You that the fruit of gentleness is just as available to me as it is to anyone else and help me to ground myself in Your love so I can grow better fruit. I want to be more like You, so please help me to live in step with Your Spirit. In Jesus's name, amen.

THINK

PRAY

PRAISE

TO-DO

PRAYER LIST

QUESTIONS FOR DEEPER REFLECTION

1. Have you convinced yourself that gentleness isn't for you because of your personality? Write down the personality traits that you feel are holding you back and pray over them.

2. What is your understanding of the Holy Spirit's role in growing in gentleness? Has it changed in the past weeks? Do you need to actively invite the Holy Spirit to grow His fruit in you? If so, do that now.

DAY 13

PURSUING GENTLENESS

But you, man of God, flee from these things, and pursue righteousness, godliness, faith, love, endurance, and gentleness.
—1 Timothy 6:11

My favorite childhood grocery store was the Real Canadian Superstore. (If you didn't already know that I live in Canada, now you do.) It wasn't my favorite because of the lobsters in tanks in the back (although they were fun to visit) or the abundance of food, but because of the roller-skating guys. Whenever a cashier needed a price check or an item changed, they'd call a roller-skating guy over and he'd zip through the store to check the item. I thought that was the most amazing job ever. Sadly, the practice was phased out in the 2000s.

But wouldn't it be great if we could access the fruit of the Spirit in the same way? I imagine myself standing in line at Superstore, struggling to be gentle with my hungry, whining child, and the cashier calls over a roller-skating guy: "Get this lady some gentleness from aisle nine! Stat!" He'd zip through the store, grab some gentleness, hand it over, and voila, I'd be a gentle person.

I used to think the fruit of the Spirit worked like that, as if God had a produce section in His warehouse and when I needed patience or gentleness, I could simply put in my order and He'd serve it up. Don't get me wrong, sometimes God really does give supernatural patience or gentleness in the moment we need it. But 1 Timothy 6:11

reminds us that we need to actively pursue a righteous life because it's not easy. Notice the verbs used in this translation:

> *But you, Timothy, man of God: Run for your life from all this. Pursue a righteous life—a life of wonder, faith, love, steadiness, courtesy. Run hard and fast in the faith. Seize the eternal life, the life you were called to, the life you so fervently embraced in the presence of so many witnesses.* —1 Timothy 6:11–12 MSG

Paul urges Timothy to run from evil and toward faith, pursue a righteous life, and seize the eternal life that he'd already embraced. You and I need to live like this too, not because it will save us, but out of gratitude for the saving grace we've already received from Jesus. Most importantly, we run, pursue, seize, and embrace through the power of the Holy Spirit in us. (Maybe we even roller-skate in His power too.)

SOMETHING TO THINK ABOUT

Imagine there's someone in your community who gets under your skin. Everything she says seems designed to annoy you. So you say, "I am determined to love her" and pray for more love, summoning all your willpower to display God's love. But it doesn't work. We aren't wrong to seek love from God. But we are wrong, Watchman Nee said, "In seeking that love as something in itself, a kind of package commodity, when what God desires is to express through you the love of His Son ... The Holy Spirit has been sent to produce what is of Christ in us."[15] As Christians, we live in this tension of needing to find our complete identity and strength in Christ, then learning to pursue a life of righteousness through the power of the Spirit.

How can we practically pursue gentleness in the middle of a culture that lives for outrage, combatting our natural tendency to lash out instead of holding our strength back for the sake of others?

First, notice the recurring situations that trigger you to speak or act ungently. Perhaps you have a neighbor who gets you riled up, a

15. Nee, *Sit, Walk, Stand*, 37.

child who knows how to push your buttons, or a certain topic on the Internet that you always type fierce comments or posts about. Are there certain situations where you tend to lift your metaphorical fists and get into a fighting stance?

Now bring those situations to God. Confess your tendency toward harshness. *"If we confess our sins, he is faithful and righteous to forgive us our sins and to cleanse us from all unrighteousness"* (1 John 1:9). Invite God to *"create a clean heart"* in you (Psalm 51:10), remembering that *"it is God who is working in you both to will and to work according to his good purpose"* (Philippians 2:13). Ask God to help you be more aware when you're close to losing control and to help you see the offending person through His eyes.

EXTRA VERSES FOR STUDY OR PRAYER

First Corinthians 9:24–27; Ephesians 3:16–19; Hebrews 12:1–2

VERSE OF THE DAY

But you, man of God, flee from these things, and pursue righteousness, godliness, faith, love, endurance, and gentleness.

—1 Timothy 6:11

PRAYER

God, please forgive me for the many times I haven't fled from evil or haven't actively pursued righteousness, godliness, faith, love, endurance, and gentleness. Please show me how to run hard and fast in this faith and to be willing to actively practice gentleness as You fill me with Your Spirit. In Jesus's name, amen.

THINK

PRAY

PRAISE

TO-DO

PRAYER LIST

QUESTIONS FOR DEEPER REFLECTION

1. What situations trigger you to speak or act ungently? Invite God to speak to you about some ways you can gain control before you lash out or use your power for ill.

2. Write out this prayer for times when you are just unable to show gentleness:

   Lord, it is clear to me at last that in myself I cannot be gentle with ____________________, but I know now that there is a life within me, the life of Your Son, and that the law of that life is to be gentle and loving. It cannot be anything but gentle. I rest in Your gentleness.[16]

16. Adapted from Nee, *Sit, Walk, Stand*, 38.

DAY 14

PUTTING ON GENTLENESS

Therefore, as God's chosen ones, holy and dearly loved, put on compassion, kindness, humility, gentleness, and patience, bearing with one another and forgiving one another if anyone has a grievance against another. Just as the Lord has forgiven you, so you are also to forgive. Above all, put on love, which is the perfect bond of unity.
—Colossians 3:12–14

One of my boys was in a *mood*, and I had no idea why. Within minutes of being in the same room, we were sniping at each other. I was immensely frustrated with the way he was speaking to me—and several minutes into the escalating argument, he wailed that he had been in pain all night, he hadn't slept well, and he was still in pain now, even after breakfast. Ooof! Had I known this before walking into the kitchen, our whole morning would have turned out very differently.

Wouldn't it be so much easier to be gentle with people if we knew exactly what pain they were experiencing? If I knew the rude person on the bus had just lost his job, the mom yelling at her kids in the grocery store was in the middle of a messy divorce, or the snarky teen at the park had an invisible disability, I could be far more gentle with each of them. It would be easier to drop the judgment and be gentle because I have empathy for them.

Unfortunately, we can't possibly know what everyone is going through or has been through, which is why most of us walk through life silently judging those around us and reacting in extremely ungentle ways. How can we live out the Bible's command to be gentle if we're living in judgment of others?

This reminds me of the woman who cried at Jesus's feet. She snuck into a dinner party and washed His dusty feet with tears of repentance, wiping them with her hair then anointing them with expensive perfume. Others at the table were judgmental of her.

> *When the Pharisee who had invited him saw this, he said to himself, "This man, if he were a prophet, would know who and what kind of woman this is who is touching him—she's a sinner!"*
>
> —Luke 7:39

Jesus did indeed know who was wiping His feet. He knew her story and how much she'd been forgiven. He accepted her offering and instead of reacting in frustration to the strange interruption to His meal, He called out His host who had perhaps deliberately slighted Him by not washing His feet or anointing His head.

Most of us are more like the Pharisee than we want to admit. We walk down the path of silent judgment, treating others harshly because we expect more from them than they're able to give. It's tough to be gentle with someone when we're silently judging them. But everyone has struggles, big and small. You may judge your daughter as cranky when she actually had a really bad day at school. You may judge your husband as moody when there's something big happening at work that he's still processing and not ready to talk about. You might judge your friend as terrible at returning your texts when she's overwhelmed with an ill parent.

What if we let Jesus walk us down a new path instead? Jesus longs to show us a new way to be human. A way that involves putting on compassion, kindness, humility, gentleness, and patience like our daily clothing. His way also involves being patient with each other and forgiving when someone wrongs us. And above all, we are to put on love as our primary identity, which will help us do all the above, leading to unity in the family of Christ.

SOMETHING TO THINK ABOUT

This way of living doesn't come naturally to us. Naturally, we live out the types of *"works of the flesh ...: sexual immorality, moral impurity, promiscuity, idolatry, sorcery, hatreds, strife, jealousy, outbursts of anger, selfish ambitions, dissensions, factions, envy, drunkenness, carousing, and anything similar"* (Galatians 5:19–21). It's only when the Spirit of Christ comes to live inside us that we can truly grow in Christlike gentleness, but He never said it would be easy. Instead, Paul warns us, *"Now those who belong to Christ Jesus have crucified the flesh with its passions and desires"* (Galatians 5:24).

Growing in the fruit of gentleness is a sign that we are crucifying our natural desire to judge others and choosing to live by the Spirit's power. You and I can't put on gentleness on our own, but with the power of the Holy Spirit backing us up, we can choose to see others through the eyes of Christ and extend gentleness instead of judgment. Even if we don't know what others are struggling with, we can empathize with them when we remember God's gentleness with us. Remembering God's care and grace in our own moments of weakness enables us to extend that same gentle response to others.

EXTRA VERSES FOR STUDY OR PRAYER

Luke 7:36–50

VERSE OF THE DAY

Therefore, as God's chosen ones, holy and dearly loved, put on compassion, kindness, humility, gentleness, and patience, bearing with one another and forgiving one another if anyone has a grievance against another. Just as the Lord has forgiven you, so you are also to forgive. Above all, put on love, which is the perfect bond of unity.

—Colossians 3:12–14

PRAYER

God, I confess the times when I've stood in judgment over someone instead of extending gentleness. Please help me to put on compassion, kindness, humility, gentleness and patience. Help me bear with others and forgive those who've hurt me. And most of all, give me the ability to put on love, through the power of Your Spirit. In Jesus's name, amen.

THINK

PRAY

PRAISE

TO-DO

PRAYER LIST

QUESTIONS FOR DEEPER REFLECTION

1. Who are you most likely to judge? Write down the thoughts you've had about that person and confess them to the Lord.

2. Imagine yourself literally clothed with the virtues mentioned in Colossians 3:12–14. How does it feel to put them on? How can you remember to put them on daily?

DAY 15

PRACTICING GENTLENESS

Remind them to submit to rulers and authorities, to obey, to be ready for every good work, to slander no one, to avoid fighting, and to be kind, always showing gentleness to all people.
—Titus 3:1–2

I drove in silence, listening to my boys bicker in the back seat. One of my boys angrily brought up something his brother had done months ago. I was shocked that he had been holding onto his anger for that long. But isn't it just so *human* of him to do so? We can see examples of this grudge fighting all over, from political conversations to the way we treat other Christians. We are angry about what's happened in the past and anxious about what might happen in future, so we are ungracious, unkind, disrespectful, and otherwise not very Christlike, both online and in person.

Titus 3:1–2 tells us to "*always* [show] *gentleness to all people.*"

The early Christians lived in a society even more opposed to them than ours is to modern Christianity. They had a target painted on their backs both by the Romans, who hated their refusal to worship Caesar as Lord, and the Jewish leaders, who disliked their belief that Jesus was the Son of God and their abandonment of the law of Moses. In fact, Paul wrote this letter to Titus around AD 63–68, when Nero was the emperor of Rome. Nero blamed Christians for the Great Fire of Rome in AD 64 and began to hunt them down so he could kill them in all sorts of cruel ways, such as burning them alive or letting them be eaten by wild animals. And yet, in his letters to Titus and the Christians in Rome, Paul reminded them to submit to their rulers. They didn't need to put an even bigger target on their backs by being intentionally disrespectful of authority.

SOMETHING TO THINK ABOUT

What does it mean to submit to rulers and authorities in a gentle manner? Surely, sometimes rulers are wrong and laws need to be changed, but the way we go about pushing for the changes is just as important as the change itself. The first thing we need to do, as followers of Christ, is to invite Him into the conversation.

> *First of all, then, I urge that petitions, prayers, intercessions, and thanksgivings be made for everyone, for kings and all those who are in authority, so that we may lead a tranquil and quiet life in all godliness and dignity. This is good, and it pleases God our Savior, who wants everyone to be saved and to come to the knowledge of the truth.* —1 Timothy 2:1–4

Assuming we're consistently praying about the situation, Titus 3:1–2 also gives us clues on how political change can be done well. First, we need to obey our rulers and authorities in humility, as long as they're not asking us to do something morally wrong. We need to be ready for every good work because "*we are his workmanship, created in Christ Jesus for good works, which God prepared ahead of time for us to do*" (Ephesians 2:10). If you're inviting Him to work, God will ask you to do something too!

Second, Titus 3 reminds us to slander no one and avoid fighting. This means we don't get to dredge up past offenses or bicker endlessly, talking in circles just to make it look like we're doing something productive. This also means we need to watch what we say online. It's far too easy to fight and slander when we're safely behind our screens, hiding in a comment section or even instigating the fights.

Finally, we are to be kind and show gentleness. In this case, I think gentleness involves both humility and respect because sometimes the hardest people to be kind and gentle to are those who seem opposed to us politically. We don't understand them, or we see the harm their policies have caused in the past, and we think they're wrong and we're right. We want to see change. But we can't solve every problem on our own, and we need to rely on God's strength and wisdom to help effect lasting change.

EXTRA VERSES FOR STUDY OR PRAYER

Romans 13:1–7; 1 Timothy 2:1–4

VERSE OF THE DAY

Remind them to submit to rulers and authorities, to obey, to be ready for every good work, to slander no one, to avoid fighting, and to be kind, always showing gentleness to all people.

—Titus 3:1–2

PRAYER

God, I confess that I've fallen far short of the way You've asked me to live. Help me to submit to the rulers and authorities around me, to obey with humility, to be ready for every good work, to avoid slander and fighting, and to be kind and gentle. May I strive to do this through Your strength, which so powerfully works in me. In Jesus's name, amen.

THINK

PRAY

PRAISE

TO-DO

PRAYER LIST

QUESTIONS FOR DEEPER REFLECTION

1. Do the people around you know you as someone who lives out Titus 3:1–2? Why or why not? Does something need to change?

2. What makes you anxious or angry about the current political climate? Take that to God in prayer and ask Him to help you follow the way of gentleness even in this.

DAY 16

JUST ENOUGH POWER

After making a whip out of cords, he drove everyone out of the temple with their sheep and oxen. He also poured out the money changers' coins and overturned the tables. He told those who were selling doves, "Get these things out of here! Stop turning my Father's house into a marketplace!"
—John 2:15–17

My toddler sat in the soft sand and giggled, grasping a yellow shovel with his chubby fingers. Laughs and shouts from other children wafted toward us on the warm summer breeze. Suddenly, a new sound cut through the joyful ones. A yapping dog leapt over the low beam around the sandbox and came straight for my son. The dog danced and barked around my little boy while he raised his hands and screamed in terror. I scooped him up, incensed that someone had let their dog run up to a small child. The owner ambled up, laughing at her dog's antics while my child bawled. I quivered with anger. I am not a confrontational person, but this had to be dealt with.

"This is *not* an off-leash park," I said firmly. The woman stopped chuckling and grabbed her dog, clearly irritated with me. Didn't I find her dog's antics hilarious? Not when they terrified my small son.

In this instance, protecting the vulnerable required me to be forceful, just like Jesus was when He walked into the temple during Passover. He had traveled far for the holy day, and like many others, He could have purchased an animal offering right there. What a great system, right? Money changers helped Jews swap their foreign coins for the right currency, and then people could purchase an ox, a sheep, or doves for their offerings right away. Those who were wealthy could afford sheep or oxen and the poor would purchase doves. But as you can imagine, every businessman wanted to make a profit—and who would be hurt the most by this system of changing money and last-minute purchases? The poor and those who had traveled from afar.

This dramatic scene is recorded slightly differently in each gospel, and together, they shed light on Jesus's motivations in this moment. Luke's Gospel gives the most basic telling, simply saying Jesus began to throw out those who were selling, telling His listeners they've turned a house of prayer into a den of thieves. (See Luke 19:45–46.) In Matthew and Mark, we get a little more detail because Jesus specifically overturns the tables of the money changers and the seats of those selling doves, targeting those who take advantage of foreigners and the poor. (See Matthew 21:12–13; Mark 11:15–16.)

John writes that Jesus walked into the temple courts, saw what was happening, and fashioned a whip out of cords before proceeding to drive out the sheep and oxen, along with their owners, pour out the money changers' coins, and overturn the tables. Then He turned His attention toward those who sold doves and said, *"Get these things out of here!"* Jesus was rightly furious that the place of worship had been turned into a place of greed and exploitation.

You're probably wondering why this passage has been included in a book on gentleness. But you see, Jesus was still holding back His power. He made a whip to drive out the animals, as was common practice, but despite copious Renaissance art that implies He used it on women and children, the Jesus we meet in the Gospels would not have used it on people. He used *just enough* power to protect the vulnerable. No more and no less than needed. He could have ordered angels to scour the temple clean of exploiters, but Jesus didn't betray His own gentle and lowly heart in a moment of impulse or emotional deregulation. He likely took time to prepare prayerfully while He wove the whip, then forcefully argued for justice while still keeping

His immense power in check. The Good Shepherd protected His sheep.

SOMETHING TO THINK ABOUT

Being gentle doesn't mean we sit idly while injustice happens around us. Rather, when we're moved to action by the problems in this world, we can take our cue from Jesus. Like Jesus, we can choose to defend the interests of those who can't defend themselves (instead of our own interests), and we can choose to uphold God's righteousness (instead of our own reputations). We can take time to prepare prayerfully, ensuring we have the heart of God in this situation, then forcefully argue for justice while using just enough power to make the point. Through the power of the Holy Spirit in us, we can find ways to respond that are loving and selfless while still truth-telling, firm and effective. It's a fine line to walk and one we tend to fall off, but we can continue to choose to turn back to our gentle-and-firm Christ for help.

EXTRA VERSES FOR STUDY OR PRAYER

Matthew 21:12–13; Mark 11:15–18; Luke 19:45–48

VERSE OF THE DAY

After making a whip out of cords, he drove everyone out of the temple with their sheep and oxen. He also poured out the money changers' coins and overturned the tables. He told those who were selling doves, "Get these things out of here! Stop turning my Father's house into a marketplace!" —John 2:15–17

PRAYER

Jesus, forgive me for the times I've thought gentleness meant inaction as well as for the times I bulldozed my way through justice issues without being tempered by Your gentleness. Break my heart for the issues that break Your heart and help me to stand up for the vulnerable with the firm passion that You displayed on earth. In Jesus's name, amen.

THINK

PRAY

PRAISE

TO-DO

PRAYER LIST

QUESTIONS FOR DEEPER REFLECTION

1. Think of a time when you stood up for someone and let your anger get the best of you. How might Jesus call you to respond differently if it happens again?

2. What group of vulnerable people stirs your heart the most today? Ask God to show you how He wants you to stand up for them.

DAY 17

GENTLENESS IN CRITICISM

For to this you have been called, because Christ also suffered for you, leaving you an example, so that you might follow in his steps. He committed no sin, neither was deceit found in his mouth. When he was reviled, he did not revile in return; when he suffered, he did not threaten, but continued entrusting himself to him who judges justly.

—1 Peter 2:21–23 (ESV)

My face grew hot with shame as I cradled the phone, listening to the woman on the other end calling me out for things I didn't even remember doing. The criticism felt unwarranted and the shock of twenty minutes of criticism caused me to start bawling. My husband came to investigate, took the phone from me, and after a short conversation with the other woman in which he told her never to speak like that to me again, he slammed the phone down. I was shaken. I had been insulted before, but never to this extent.

Jesus knows exactly what it feels like to be criticized and insulted. When Nathanael first met Jesus, he wondered if "*anything good*" could come out of Jesus's hometown of Nazareth (John 1:46). Pharisees criticized Jesus for disobeying their interpretation of God's law and accused Him of being in league with the devil. (See Matthew 9:34.) During His rigged trial, Jesus was mocked and insulted by priests, politicians, and soldiers. Jesus understood rejection, rudeness, and disrespect.

But instead of pushing Nathanael away, Jesus complimented him. (See John 1:47.) Jesus taught those who misunderstood Him, kept on driving out demons and healing the sick, and rebuked His disciples for their thirst for vengeance. During His trial, Jesus stood His ground, quietly taking the insults and mockery that came at Him. Because Jesus was fully human, this must have been just as hard for Him as it would be for you and me.

Hebrews 4:15 says, *"We do not have a high priest who is unable to sympathize with our weaknesses, but one who has been tempted in every way as we are, yet without sin."* Jesus could have lashed out, but instead:

> *"He committed no sin, and no deceit was found in his mouth." When they hurled their insults at him, he did not retaliate; when he suffered, he made no threats. Instead, he entrusted himself to him who judges justly.* —1 Peter 2:22–23 NIV

Jesus isn't our only biblical example of responding to criticism with gentleness. When David's son Absalom tried to take his father's throne, David and his family fled. Along the way, they passed Shimei, a man who was related to the previous king. Shimei threw stones at David and his entourage, cursing them as they went past, saying:

> *The LORD has paid you back for all the blood of the house of Saul in whose place you became king, and the LORD has handed the kingdom over to your son Absalom. Look, you are in trouble because you're a man of bloodshed!* —2 Samuel 16:8

One of David's men was deeply insulted and begged his permission to cut off Shimei's head. Rather than allowing his vengeful soldier to have his way, David told him, *"Leave him alone and let him curse me; the LORD has told him to. Perhaps the LORD will see my affliction and restore goodness to me instead of Shimei's curses today"* (2 Samuel 16:11–12). David and his family and friends simply kept walking as

Shimei continued to curse them, throw stones, and kick up dust at them.

SOMETHING TO THINK ABOUT

Both David and Jesus trusted themselves to the One who judges justly, placing their need for retaliation in the hands of the gracious Judge instead of trying to take it on themselves. You and I can also trust God to defend us when appropriate. We can lay down our defensive responses to criticism when we allow God to be the Judge.

I hope you haven't been verbally cursed or accused of being in league with the devil, but I guarantee you'll feel insulted, slighted, or outraged at some point in your life. But if we want to truly grow in gentleness, we have to learn to be gentle in the little things before we'll be able to be as gentle as Jesus with a big enemy.

Oh, and the end of my story? My husband didn't think I had anything to apologize for, but the next time that woman called, I swiftly apologized for the things I realized I had actually done. The courageous gentleness the Holy Spirit gave me in that moment completely disarmed her and turned our relationship around. Choosing gentleness allowed for the power of God to move in my relationship.

EXTRA VERSES FOR STUDY OR PRAYER

Second Samuel 16:5–14

VERSE OF THE DAY

For to this you have been called, because Christ also suffered for you, leaving you an example, so that you might follow in his steps. He committed no sin, neither was deceit found in his mouth. When he was reviled, he did not revile in return; when he suffered, he did not threaten, but continued entrusting himself to him who judges justly. —1 Peter 2:21–23 (ESV)

PRAYER

Jesus, thank You for suffering for me and leaving an example so I can follow in Your steps. Please help me to keep my retorts and insults to myself and reshape my mind so I can completely trust myself to You, who judges justly. In Jesus's name, amen.

THINK

PRAY

PRAISE

TO-DO

PRAYER LIST

QUESTIONS FOR DEEPER REFLECTION

1. Describe a time you were insulted or criticized. What emotions did you feel? How did you deal with it?

2. Write out 1 Peter 2:21–23 from your favorite Bible translation and invite God to work in your heart as you write.

DAY 18

RESISTING GENTLY

But I say to you who listen: Love your enemies, do what is good to those who hate you, bless those who curse you, pray for those who mistreat you.
—Luke 6:27–28

Corrie ten Boom, part of the Dutch resistance during World War II, was asked by the underground movement to help them find an assassin. They wanted to eliminate someone in the police department who was leaking information to the Gestapo. It was critical, they said, to eliminate this double agent before he could cause more pain and destruction. It seemed like a reasonable request for the middle of wartime, especially when we look back on the atrocities of the Nazi regime. However, Corrie chose not to participate. Instead, she prayed for the betraying Dutchman, asking that he would know his own worth in the sight of God, as well as the worth of every person.[17] Corrie's life consistently showed the power of God's radical gentleness by living out Jesus's command to *"love your enemies and pray for those who persecute you"* (Matthew 5:44).

Maybe it's just me, but I think Jesus's words on how we are to treat our enemies are some of the hardest teachings to live out. Jesus told His followers very clearly, *"don't resist an evildoer. On the contrary, if anyone slaps you on your right cheek, turn the other to him also"* (Matthew 5:39). But Jesus didn't just preach this life of non-violence;

17. Larry Loftis, *The Watchmaker's Daughter: The True Story of World War II Heroine Corrie ten Boom* (New York: HarperCollins, 2023), chapter 11, "The Mission."

He lived out His own message. After His arrest, Jesus didn't resist anyone on the way to the cross. The Word of God allowed Himself to be stripped and beaten, the King of Kings allowed Himself to be spat upon and dragged through the streets, and the Only Begotten who holds the name above all names allowed Himself to be mocked by a name placed above His cross. We might say, "Well, that's just because He had to die for our sins," but the New Testament is filled with disciples and apostles changing their world by pointing to God's power instead of forcing their own.

Jesus's words weren't just for one time and place. They were for all followers, everywhere. The kingdom of God is a different kind of kingdom—not one of bloodshed and violence, but one where enemies are given extra coats and money and food. Jesus's kingdom is filled with people who choose to faithfully hold back their own power for the sake of the vulnerable and weak, so that they can get to know our gentle and lowly Savior.

SOMETHING TO THINK ABOUT

I've never been arrested on trumped-up charges, nor have I needed to fight an evil authority. While my enemies may not be as obvious or the consequences as deadly, I still need to ask the Holy Spirit to help me love the enemies I do have. That might look like choosing not to engage in a comment-section debate on Instagram or retaliate against an atheist who says my family discipleship work consists of brainwashing kids. Sometimes it seems like the super-opinionated woman at church, my uncle, or even my own child feels like my enemy. What has Jesus called me to do? Don't resist an evildoer. Pray for those who persecute me. Turn the other cheek. Give to those who want to borrow from me. In short, "*Be merciful, just as your Father also is merciful*" (Luke 6:36).

Acting in gentleness may not help me win the person over or change the situation. Early on in the civil rights movement, Philip Yancey thought Martin Luther King Jr. and the protesters were wrong. "I was quick to pounce on his moral flaws and slow to recognize my own blind sin," Yancey wrote. "But because he stayed faithful, by offering his body as a target but never as a weapon, he broke through my moral calluses."[18]

Sometimes gentleness wins and my enemy's heart is changed. Other times, it won't seem to change anything except my own heart. But we don't treat our enemies with gentleness so we can win; we do it out of faithfulness to Jesus. He commands us to "*love your enemies, do what is good, and lend, expecting nothing in return*" (Luke 6:35). And His promise? "*Then your reward will be great, and you will be children of the Most High.*" What greater reward could there be?

EXTRA VERSES FOR STUDY OR PRAYER

Proverbs 9:7–9; Matthew 5:38–48; Luke 6:27–36

VERSE OF THE DAY

But I say to you who listen: Love your enemies, do what is good to those who hate you, bless those who curse you, pray for those who mistreat you. —Luke 6:27–28

PRAYER

Jesus, this is a hard teaching. Thank You for not leaving me to work on this on my own, but for giving me Your Spirit to help me live this out. Help me to love my enemies and do what is good to those who hate or dislike me. Teach me to bless those who curse me and pray for those who mistreat me. In Jesus's name, amen.

THINK

18. Philip Yancey, *The Jesus I Never Knew* (Grand Rapids, MI: Zondervan, 1995), 122.

PRAY

PRAISE

TO-DO

PRAYER LIST

QUESTIONS FOR DEEPER REFLECTION

1. Who has felt like an enemy recently?

2. How is Jesus calling you to live out His teachings with that enemy? Do you need to turn the other cheek? Give to someone who's asking? Bless someone who's cursed you or pray for one who has mistreated you?

DAY 19

VENGEANCE IS THE LORD'S

Do not be conquered by evil, but conquer evil with good.
—Romans 12:21

I hadn't heard of Daryl Davis until his story came across my Facebook feed, but it didn't take more than a glance before I was pulled into his dramatic story of conquering evil with good. Davis is a black musician, author, and Christian who befriended members of the Ku Klux Klan and other white supremacist groups. Through listening, patience, and caring for others, he developed genuine friendships with those who were committed to hating him. Davis ate with them, played music with them, and attended their family weddings. As a result of his friendship, many renounced their racism and ties to the KKK, even giving him their ceremonial robes as a sign of their change of heart.[19]

The way Davis behaved with his friends went far beyond simple kindness. By laying down of the need for vengeance, he was able to live out Romans 12:18–21 (ESV):

> *If possible, so far as it depends on you, live peaceably with all. Beloved, never avenge yourselves, but leave it to the wrath of God, for it is written, "Vengeance is mine, I will repay, says the*

19. Daryl Davis's story is told in the documentary *Accidental Courtesy: Daryl Davis, Race & America*, directed by Matthew Ornstein (2016; First Run Features); Daryl Davis, *Klan-Destine Relationships: A Black Man's Odyssey in the Ku Klux Klan* (Far Hills, NJ: New Horizon Press, 2005); and his website www.daryldavis.com.

> *Lord." To the contrary, "if your enemy is hungry, feed him; if he is thirsty, give him something to drink; for by so doing you will heap burning coals on his head." Do not be overcome by evil, but overcome evil with good.*

One of the ultimate goals of gentleness is that we might conquer evil with good. This is exactly what Jesus did when He went willingly to the cross then walked out of the tomb, but we even see hints of God's plan for this type of living in the Old Testament.

In 2 Kings 6, the king of Aram is incredibly frustrated with Elisha. In a supernatural game of telephone, Elisha passes on messages from God about the Arameans' battle plans to the king of Israel. The Aramean king decides to take God's messenger out of the equation by sending a battalion to capture Elisha. In the morning, Elisha's servant discovers the entire city surrounded by enemy chariots. He panics, but Elisha prays for him, and he's suddenly able to see the hills full of an angel army sent by God to protect Elisha. But the prophet doesn't use his power to kill the Arameans; instead, he prays for them to become temporarily blinded.

Then, Elisha leads them to Samaria, into the court of the king of Israel. Elisha prays for their eyes to be opened and the huge force of Israel's enemies can suddenly see again, only to discover they are now the ones who are surrounded. The king of Israel asks Elisha, *"Should I kill them, should I kill them, my father?"* (2 Kings 6:21). In this moment, Elisha gives us a clue as to what God plans to do through Jesus. He tells the king to feed his enemies, so they are given a big feast and then sent on their way. In an incredible twist, Israel's gentleness in this moment led the Arameans to stop raiding Israel's territory.

SOMETHING TO THINK ABOUT

We've been working under a definition of gentleness that says, "Gentleness is holding back my power for the sake of the vulnerable," but we can also look at it as exercising God's strength with God's self-control. The power isn't mine to begin with; it's God's power. Something I read in a YouVersion devotional rings so true:

> It's understanding and valuing power because you know that true power only comes from God, that apart from Him we can do nothing, and that He has been and continues to be gentle with us. And because you have this understanding, you cling to compassion rather than anger; you act—and react—as Christ did, without undue harshness, responding instead with kindness, sincerity, and love.[20]

You may not have an army camped on your doorstep, but there are likely areas of your life where it seems like evil is winning. As we see in the example of Elisha and the Arameans as well as the example of Daryl Davis and the KKK, practicing gentleness in the power of Christ leads to peace. Not a pretend, fake-smile type of peace, but a true peace that causes ripples of change in the world.

EXTRA VERSES FOR STUDY OR PRAYER

Second Kings 6:8–23; Romans 12:18–21

VERSE OF THE DAY

Do not be conquered by evil, but conquer evil with good.

—Romans 12:21

PRAYER

God, there is nothing easy about conquering evil with good, but I know that through the power of Your incredible gentleness, You conquered evil for all time. While I live in the here-but-not-yet period of Your kingdom, please help me to be an example of Your gentleness in the world, bringing peace to relationships and hearts. Allow me to cause change that ripples through my community. In Jesus's name, amen.

---

20. Calgary Chapel Fort Lauderdale, YouVersion Bible app *Fruit of the Spirit: Gentleness,* day 3 "Meek and Gentle" by Danny Saavedra, www.bible.com/reading-plans/38031-fruit-of-the-spirit-gentleness.

THINK

PRAY

PRAISE

TO-DO

PRAYER LIST

QUESTIONS FOR DEEPER REFLECTION

1. In what area of your life do you find it hard to live at peace with others? How might choosing gentleness make a difference in that area?

2. Prayerfully reread Romans 12:18–21. Ask God what He wants you to pay extra attention to today. Write down any thoughts.

DAY 20

TRUSTING MEEKNESS

Blessed are the meek, for they shall inherit the earth.
—Matthew 5:5 (ESV)

David and his men huddled in the back of the cave, breathing as quietly as possible. Their enemy, Saul, David's father-in-law and the king of Israel, stood just outside the cave, talking loudly to his men.

"Stay alert. I won't be long." Soon, someone shuffled toward David's silent men, then stopped. They were incredulous: the king had just put himself in a vulnerable position and was without his guard. They said to David, *"Look, this is the day the LORD told you about: 'I will hand your enemy over to you so you can do to him whatever you desire'"* (1 Samuel 24:4). David crept toward the man who had hunted him for months, but instead of using his weapon to kill the king, he used it to cut off a corner of his robe.

Afterward, David felt so guilty, he chased Saul down, bowed low, and confessed what he had nearly done. He knew he couldn't kill God's anointed king, no matter how badly he had been treated. He told Saul, *"May the LORD judge between me and you, and may the LORD take vengeance on you for me, but my hand will never be against you"* (1 Samuel 24:12). We've defined this holding back of power as gentleness, but it's also translated as "meekness" in the Bible. The Outline of Bible Usage describes the meek as "those wholly relying on God rather than their own strength to defend against injustice ... Gentleness or meekness is the opposite to self-assertiveness and self-interest. It stems from trust in God's goodness and control over the situation."[21] Every time David chose to rely on God rather than his own strength, God was able to prove his own power, bringing Saul to the realization that he had done wrong to David.

In 2 Samuel 22:36 (ESV), David prayed, *"You have given me the shield of your salvation, and your gentleness made me great."* David knew that he was made great because of God's gentle strength and redemption, not because of David's own wits or strength. He didn't need to be self-assertive in order to become king. David refused to take something that didn't belong to him because gentleness opposes *taking*. Instead, he recognized what God had *given*. In the end, David did inherit the kingdom of Israel, not by assassinating the king, but by choosing to trust God's goodness and control over the situation.

SOMETHING TO THINK ABOUT

While David was hiding from Saul in a cave, he composed this psalm:

> *Be gracious to me, God, be gracious to me, for I take refuge in you. I will seek refuge in the shadow of your wings until danger passes. I call to God Most High, to God who fulfills his purpose for me.* —Psalm 57:1–2

David knew he didn't need to force Saul off the throne of Israel. He simply needed to take refuge in the shadow of his Father's wings. It wasn't always easy to do, as evidenced by David's complaint a few verses late: *"They prepared a net for my steps; I was despondent"* (verse 6). He knew his enemy was closing in, but still he trusted, crying out, *"They dug a pit ahead of me, but they fell into it!"* David was ultimately vindicated by God Himself and didn't need to resort to brute strength or assassination to take hold of the promised throne.

In David's case, as in Jesus's, the way to true power lay through the path of meekness. Jesus says the same truth applies to us in the Beatitudes of Matthew 5. He teaches the unconventional truth that the meek *"shall inherit the earth."* But in order to live in Christlike

21. www.blueletterbible.org/lexicon/g4239/kjv/tr/0-1.

meekness, we have to recognize what weapons we actually need to be fighting our battles with. We don't need weapons in our hands; we just need to lift our hands in prayer. In 2 Corinthians 10:3–4, Paul reminds us:

> *Although we live in the flesh, we do not wage war according to the flesh, since the weapons of our warfare are not of the flesh, but are powerful through God for the demolition of strongholds.*

The weapons of our warfare are prayer and faith in God, who is just. In faith, we can trust that God will fight on our behalf. We can wholly rely on God rather than our own strength to defend against injustice in our lives and in the lives of those we help. We trust that Jesus was telling the truth when He said we would inherit the earth by being fully surrendered to His power and plan, just as David surrendered to God's plan to get him on the throne of Israel.

EXTRA VERSES FOR STUDY OR PRAYER

Psalm 57; 1 Peter 5:6–7

VERSE OF THE DAY

Blessed are the meek, for they shall inherit the earth.

—Matthew 5:5 (ESV)

PRAYER

Jesus, You promised that the meek are blessed and will inherit the earth. I trust in Your promise, fully surrendering myself to Your power and plan. Please do the hard work of changing hearts as I take refuge in You and allow You to fight my biggest battles for me. In Jesus's name, amen.

THINK

PRAY

PRAISE

TO-DO

PRAYER LIST

QUESTIONS FOR DEEPER REFLECTION

1. Is there a situation you need to give to God today?

2. Do you feel meek today? What's holding you back from truly living in meekness?

DAY 21

GENTLE LEADERSHIP

Brothers and sisters, if someone is overtaken in any wrongdoing, you who are spiritual, restore such a person with a gentle spirit, watching out for yourselves so that you also won't be tempted. Carry one another's burdens; in this way you will fulfill the law of Christ.
—Galatians 6:1–2

I was excited to have my son cornered, trapped in the car with just me while I drove him to his morning program. "Perfect," I thought. "I can force a confession out of him by refusing to drop him off until he comes clean!"

You're probably cringing, and thanks be to God, I did not follow through with that plan because I doubt any confession that came under those conditions would have been honest. After a heartfelt conversation in the car that still did not elicit a confession, I remembered that if God's kindness is supposed to lead us to repentance (see Romans 2:4), my harshness certainly wasn't going to cause a change of heart. If God Himself chooses not to be harsh with me, I definitely need to be gentle when correcting my young son. He had been overtaken in wrongdoing, but my job as his mom was to restore him with a gentle spirit. Instead of cornering him into confession, I parked, invited him to hop into the front seat, then took his hands and prayed with him.

You may not be disciplining a young child these days, but the reminders in our verses today have many applications in leadership.

We often see Christians calling out or canceling wrongdoers instead of gently restoring them, and it's time to step into our calling. Galatians 6:1 explicitly calls out *"you who are spiritual"* as those who are to restore the fallen. Being spiritual in the context of the New Testament isn't just about believing in God, but about being responsive to the guidance of the Holy Spirit. As Christians, if we are truly growing in Christ, we ought to be growing in our ability to respond to the Holy Spirit's guidance, which is exactly what we need to bring a repentant wrongdoer into restorative community—one of the toughest roles of a leader.

SOMETHING TO THINK ABOUT

Jesus gave us the ultimate standard for leadership when He told His disciples:

> *You know that the rulers of the Gentiles lord it over them, and those in high positions act as tyrants over them. It must not be like that among you. On the contrary, whoever wants to become great among you must be your servant, and whoever wants to be first among you must be your slave; just as the Son of Man did not come to be served, but to serve, and to give his life as a ransom for many.* —Matthew 20:25–28

Jesus not only told us what true leadership looks like, He also modeled it and equips us to live it out through the power of His Spirit.

What else does the Bible tell us about the kind of leadership God expects to see among His people? First Timothy 3:2–3 shares the qualifications of an overseer (also translated as bishop or church leader), and again, gentleness makes the list: *"An overseer, therefore, must be above reproach, the husband of one wife, self-controlled, sensible, respectable, hospitable, able to teach, not an excessive drinker, not a bully but gentle, not quarrelsome, not greedy."*

As always, gentleness is about holding back one's power for the sake of the vulnerable. You may not hold an official leadership position in a church, but you are a leader of someone. Perhaps you lead a book club or a group of nurses in a hospital ward. Perhaps you lead kids at lunch hour or coach teens to play soccer. Even the least authoritative person usually has someone who looks to them.

So what will you do with your influence? Will you choose harshness? Or will you choose to carry the burdens of your people, gently restoring, teaching, and serving like Christ?

EXTRA VERSES FOR STUDY OR PRAYER

Matthew 20:25–28; 1 Timothy 3:2–3

VERSE OF THE DAY

Brothers and sisters, if someone is overtaken in any wrongdoing, you who are spiritual, restore such a person with a gentle spirit, watching out for yourselves so that you also won't be tempted. Carry one another's burdens; in this way you will fulfill the law of Christ. —Galatians 6:1–2

PRAYER

God, thank You for the big and small positions of leadership You've given me. Help me to not take that for granted, but to live by the Spirit in whatever role You want me in. Please help me to be gentle when I'm called to bring a wrongdoer into restoration, to teach, or to lead in any way. Help me figure out what gentleness looks like practically in my unique life. In Jesus's name, amen.

THINK

PRAY

PRAISE

TO-DO

PRAYER LIST

QUESTIONS FOR DEEPER REFLECTION

1. Have you ever had an experience of either being confronted about a sin or confronting someone else about a sin? Did you feel like it was done in gentleness? If it wasn't, invite God to speak to you about how it could go differently next time.

2. We have to be responsive to the Spirit (spiritual) to restore a person with a gentle spirit. Does that describe you? If not, invite God to help you learn to be more responsive to His Spirit.

DAY 22

BITING AND DEVOURING

For the whole law is fulfilled in one word: "You shall love your neighbor as yourself." But if you bite and devour one another, watch out that you are not consumed by one another.
—Galatians 5:14–15 (ESV)

When my sister was in high school, she conducted an experiment with mice. Much to my mother's chagrin, she brought them home for several days. One morning, we woke up to a gruesome sight: some of the mice had eaten the head of one of their cage-mates. (I told you it was gruesome.) When I read Galatians 5:15, I remember those mice: *"If you bite and devour one another, watch out, or you will be consumed by one another."* It certainly gives new meaning to the phrase, "Don't bite my head off"!

How often do we metaphorically bite and devour one another though? When we hunt for and call out any hint of heresy or hypocrisy in the Christian leaders we follow online, we bite and devour our brothers and sisters in Christ. When we nitpick at our kids for everything, we bite and devour them. When we nag our husbands or bicker with our mothers-in-law, we bite and devour. When we do this, we need to watch out because we are doing the exact opposite of Christ's command to love our neighbors as ourselves. Gentleness, as a practical act of love, is often contrasted with being quarrelsome in the New Testament letters.

Instead of living like caged mice, constantly on the verge of biting off someone else's head in a fight, we can choose to practice gentleness. As James reminds us, *"Everyone should be quick to listen, slow to speak, and slow to anger, for human anger does not accomplish God's righteousness"* (James 1:19–20). For some of us, keeping our mouths closed is the ultimate act of love, helping us to hold back a biting word for the sake of someone else. This is one way to live out Christ-centered gentleness in a world drowning in venomous words.

Refusing to quarrel isn't easy, but it is possible. Genesis 26:14–22 records a moment in time when the Philistines were so jealous of Isaac's immense wealth that they filled his father Abraham's old wells with dirt while he was away. When Isaac returned, he reopened the wells and also had his servants dig in the valley, where they came upon a well of spring water. But the herdsman living there said, *"The water is ours!"* Isaac was very wealthy and could have fought back, but instead, he named the well "Argument" and walked away from it. He dug another well. The same herdsmen quarreled with him over that well too, so he named this one "Hostility" and walked away again. Finally, after digging a third well, the local herdsmen left him alone.

Instead of feeling like a doormat, Isaac praised God and named this third well "Open Spaces," saying, *"For now the LORD has made space for us, and we will be fruitful in the land"* (Genesis 26:22). Isaac walked away from those who wanted to quarrel with him, and God rewarded him with peace. Isaac trusted God to bring justice in the situation, choosing to allow God to fight for him instead of quarreling over the wells.

SOMETHING TO THINK ABOUT

Sometimes we don't intend to be quarrelsome but seem constantly embroiled in arguments against our will. Second Timothy 2:23–26 gives us some insight on how to walk away from quarrels, what to do instead, and what God can do with our gentle responses:

> *But reject foolish and ignorant disputes, because you know that they breed quarrels. The Lord's servant must not quarrel, but*

> *must be gentle to everyone, able to teach, and patient, instructing his opponents with gentleness. Perhaps God will grant them repentance leading them to the knowledge of the truth. Then they may come to their senses and escape the trap of the devil, who has taken them captive to do his will.*

Notice that Paul is urging Timothy to give others a double helping of gentleness: *"The Lord's servant must not quarrel, but must be **gentle** to everyone . . . instructing his opponents with **gentleness**."* In this way, his listeners will repent and know Christ.

Isn't this our ultimate goal in this life? To help others come to their senses and escape the trap of the devil? Suddenly, making the choice to step out of quarrels and into gentleness seems like a small price to pay for the freedom of my friends and family.

EXTRA VERSES FOR STUDY OR PRAYER

Second Timothy 2:22–26; James 3:13–14; 1 Peter 3:16

VERSE OF THE DAY

> *For the whole law is fulfilled in one word: "You shall love your neighbor as yourself." But if you bite and devour one another, watch out that you are not consumed by one another.*
>
> —Galatians 5:14–15 (ESV)

PRAYER

Jesus, I'm so sorry for all the times I've willingly participated in a quarrel. Please help me to stop biting and devouring those around me and choose to love my neighbor as myself instead. I'm really going to need Your help with this! In Jesus's name, amen.

THINK

PRAY

PRAISE

TO-DO

PRAYER LIST

QUESTIONS FOR DEEPER REFLECTION

1. Who are you most likely to quarrel with? Why are you more prone to quarreling with this particular person? Invite God to open your heart to His insights and ask Him for courage to step away from the quarreling.

2. Is there someone in your life who draws you into quarrels? Invite God to give you ideas on how you could walk away from those situations.

DAY 23

GENTLE EVANGELISM

But even if you should suffer for righteousness' sake, you will be blessed. Have no fear of them, nor be troubled, but in your hearts honor Christ the Lord as holy, always being prepared to make a defense to anyone who asks you for a reason for the hope that is in you; yet do it with gentleness and respect, having a good conscience, so that, when you are slandered, those who revile your good behavior in Christ may be put to shame.

—1 Peter 3:14–16 (ESV)

My mentor, Mindy, and I scanned the university cafeteria, looking for someone to share the gospel with. This was my first time doing such blatant evangelism and I was thoroughly queasy. We sat down with a female student and engaged her in conversation, but once we started talking about matters of faith, it did not go well. The two of us argued over the veracity of Christianity like it was the final championships of the debate club, and Mindy and I left the table soon afterward. I was embarrassed and angry, and I'm sure we left the student feeling even more sour about people of faith.

Quietly, Mindy spoke something that has stuck with me to this day. "You can't argue someone into faith." I had missed a key part of Peter's instructions on sharing our faith with others: "*Do it with gentleness and respect*" (1 Peter 3:15 ESV).

By allowing the conversation to devolve into emotional arguments, I lost all connection to gentleness and respect (or reverence as some translations call this winning combination). From that moment on, I backed completely off from any evangelism efforts, worried that my attempt to *"make a defense"* would lead to similar souring encounters.

We want others to know the freedom that comes from knowing and following Jesus, but the way we communicate it matters deeply. As Paul teaches in 1 Corinthians 13:2, *"If I have the gift of prophecy and understand all mysteries and all knowledge, and if I have all faith so that I can move mountains but do not have love, I am nothing."* So to rephrase today's passage, "If I give a defense of my faith to anyone who asks me about the hope that is in me, but don't do it with gentleness and respect, I am nothing." If we want our words about Christ to mean something to others, we have to act like Him—or at least be growing in our ability to act like Him. We need to be able to share the gospel with our broken world in the same spirit of gentleness that Jesus *lived* the gospel.

SOMETHING TO THINK ABOUT

First Peter makes clear the connection between gentleness and respect. It's tough to be gentle with someone we don't respect, isn't it? If I had respected the anonymous woman I was trying to evangelize, I likely would have spent some time actually getting to know her before trying to convert her.

Darin and Joy Stevens from the ministry Start to Stir[22] have discovered a better way to have gospel conversations. Through many discussions, they've found that people around them aren't against God as much as they have no idea what relevance God has for their lives. So rather than having an apologetic or theological defense, Darin and Joy have begun to listen to their friends and neighbors to find out what they actually believe. They ask questions and respect both their friends' views as well as their ability to think and seek. In an Instagram post, Joy writes, "My listening created space for them to ask me what I thought and I actually had better conversations about Jesus because they were interested in what I thought as well.

22. www.starttostir.com.

Maybe the bravest thing you can do to share the gospel right now is to listen to where your friends are starting from."[23] Let's be women who choose respect and gentleness in our relationships with friends and coworkers.

EXTRA VERSES FOR STUDY OR PRAYER

First Corinthians 13:1–7

VERSE OF THE DAY

But even if you should suffer for righteousness' sake, you will be blessed. Have no fear of them, nor be troubled, but in your hearts honor Christ the Lord as holy, always being prepared to make a defense to anyone who asks you for a reason for the hope that is in you; yet do it with gentleness and respect, having a good conscience, so that, when you are slandered, those who revile your good behavior in Christ may be put to shame.

—1 Peter 3:14–16 (ESV)

PRAYER

Jesus, You are the hope inside me! Please forgive me for the times I haven't been ready to give a defense with gentleness and respect. Help me learn to speak clearly about the hope You've given me and please also help me to share it with others through gentleness. Give me the bold, compassionate love needed to point others to You. In Jesus's name, amen.

THINK

23. www.instagram.com/starttostir, March 16, 2024.

PRAY

PRAISE

TO-DO

PRAYER LIST

QUESTIONS FOR DEEPER REFLECTION

1. Can you think of a time you gave someone a defense of your faith and it didn't go over very well? What was missing—your defense, gentleness, or respect?

2. Invite God to help you grow in that area.

DAY 24

GENTLE TONGUES

No foul language should come from your mouth,
but only what is good for building up someone in need,
so that it gives grace to those who hear.
—Ephesians 4:29

Three other desks stood with mine, making a nice, neat rectangle near the edge of the third grade classroom. The teacher assigned us a task to do as a group. I took charge of the project until one boy decided he didn't like my leadership. His words still ring deep in my heart: "Stop being so bossy!" The names didn't end there. When I was in sixth grade, teachers called me quiet. When I was in junior high, boys called me ugly and girls called me shy. When I was in high school, a parent called me critical. These are all names that have been put on me at some point in my life.

What words or names have people thrown at you? Maybe the name-calling mostly happens inside your own head because your worst critic is yourself. Or perhaps you have cruel words from a parent on replay inside your mind. Those words and names change us, even define us. Years after the "bossy" incident, I realized that at that moment, I stopped being bossy. Maybe you could see that as a good thing, but in doing so, I squelched my leadership skills for many years. Had I known that my third grade bossiness was a gift from God in disguise, I might be so much further along in becoming who God created me to be. It took me years to get over those names and identities others gave me. One by one, God is washing me clean of all those words and labels, giving me a new identity based on Him.

But what happens when we're the ones pegging the labels on others? If you've never labeled someone in a fit of frustration or called them a name you later regret, I'd like to meet you because you're likely the most gentle person ever. James wrote about how incredibly hard it is to be gentle with our words:

> *So too, though the tongue is a small part of the body, it boasts great things. Consider how a small fire sets ablaze a large forest. And the tongue is a fire. The tongue, a world of unrighteousness, is placed among our members. It stains the whole body, sets the course of life on fire, and is itself set on fire by hell. Every kind of animal, bird, reptile, and fish is tamed and has been tamed by humankind, but no one can tame the tongue. It is a restless evil, full of deadly poison. With the tongue we bless our Lord and Father, and with it we curse people who are made in God's likeness. Blessing and cursing come out of the same mouth. My brothers and sisters, these things should not be this way.*
>
> —James 3:5–10

Do you ever feel like your own tongue is setting fire to the relationships and people around you, or maybe to your own identity? If so, it's time to invite the Spirit to work gentleness into your words. Because as James says about blessing and cursing coming from the same mouth, "*Does a spring pour out sweet and bitter water from the same opening? Can a fig tree produce olives, my brothers and sisters, or a grapevine produce figs? Neither can a saltwater spring yield fresh water*" (James 3:11–12). If you are filled with the Spirit of Christ, your tongue should be morphing from a place of bitterness and fire into a place where sweet, fresh words can flow, producing the kind of words that build up others and give grace to those who hear.

SOMETHING TO THINK ABOUT

Using gentle words doesn't mean we need to lie, be fake, or sugar-coat the truth. It does mean that our language needs to be humble and compassionate. Colossians 4:6 tells us, *"Let your speech always be gracious, seasoned with salt, so that you may know how you should answer each person."* When the Spirit helps us grow in gracious speech, we'll become the kind of people who build others up instead of labeling them or tearing them down. Our tongues will become like the one described in Proverbs 15:4 (ESV): *"A gentle tongue is a tree of life."* May we become known as the people with life-giving tongues.

EXTRA VERSES FOR STUDY OR PRAYER

Proverbs 15:4; Ephesians 4:15; Colossians 4:6

VERSE OF THE DAY

No foul language should come from your mouth, but only what is good for building up someone in need, so that it gives grace to those who hear. —Ephesians 4:29

PRAYER

Jesus, I'm sorry for the times when my words have been foul, hurtful, bitter, or harsh toward others and toward myself. Thank You for Your incredible, unmerited forgiveness. Please help me to speak gracious words that build others up and give grace to those who hear instead of words that only make me feel better for the moment. In Jesus's name, amen.

THINK

PRAY

PRAISE

TO-DO

PRAYER LIST

QUESTIONS FOR DEEPER REFLECTION

1. Who have you been speaking harshly to recently? (That someone might be yourself!)

2. What words does that person need to hear? Invite God to impress encouraging words and thoughts on your heart and write down what comes to mind.

DAY 25

GENTLE WISDOM

But the wisdom from above is first pure, then peace-loving, gentle, compliant, full of mercy and good fruits, unwavering, without pretense.
—James 3:17

My husband and I criticized our friends' house all the way home from dinner there. Although their home was spacious, clean, and well-decorated, we said it was too big for us. The ceiling was too high. We wouldn't want to clean it. How could they have bought such a big home? Underlying all our criticisms lay a deep well of jealousy that these friends had managed to purchase a home much more expensive than ours.

King Saul would have understood our frustrations. After all, he was the very first royal leader of the new kingdom of Israel and fully expected to pass down his rule to his son, Jonathan. But then his son's best friend defeated the enemy even Saul was too scared to confront, and the people began to sing about Israel's win against the Philistines with a song: *"Saul has killed his thousands, but David his tens of thousands"* (1 Samuel 18:7).

Instead of honoring David for trusting God, Saul descended into a deep well of jealousy that would color the rest of his life. James writes about how *"envy and selfish ambition"* lead to *"disorder and every evil practice"* (James 3:16), and Saul's remaining time in power puts this principle on full display. Because of this jealousy, he pushed away his son and daughter, both of whom loved David. He also spent more time chasing David around Israel than actually defending and leading the country. In a fit of jealous rage, he ordered the slaughter of an entire village of priests and their families. (See 1 Samuel 22:17–19.) Saul's poor leadership caused hundreds of Israelite men to join David in the wilderness instead of working with Saul to fight their common enemy, the Philistines. In the end, Saul's jealous, clutching leadership style led his fledgling kingdom to defeat.

On the other hand, Saul's son displayed a different heart.

> *Jonathan made a covenant with David because he loved him as much as himself. Then Jonathan removed the robe he was wearing and gave it to David, along with his military tunic, his sword, his bow, and his belt.* —1 Samuel 18:3–4

Instead of seeing David as a rival for the throne, Jonathan welcomed David as his best friend, protected him from his father's rage, and encouraged him in the wilderness. In a surprising turn, Jonathan even acknowledged David's God-given claim to the throne, saying, *"You yourself will be king over Israel, and I'll be your second-in-command. Even my father Saul knows it is true"* (1 Samuel 23:17). Jonathan discovered the same thing I did after I recognized how jealous I was of my friend's house and began to thank God for the gifts He had given her instead:

> *But if you have bitter envy and selfish ambition in your heart, don't boast and deny the truth. Such wisdom does not come down from above but is earthly, unspiritual, demonic. For where there is envy and selfish ambition, there is disorder and every evil practice. But the wisdom from above is first pure, then peace-loving, gentle, compliant, full of mercy and good fruits, unwavering, without pretense.* —James 3:14–17

SOMETHING TO THINK ABOUT

Bitter envy and selfish ambition are the antithesis of the kind of wisdom that comes from God. Envy causes disorder and pain and ruins relationships, but God's wisdom teaches us to hold back on our power for the sake of our relationships with others. The good news is, *"If any of you lacks wisdom, he should ask God—who gives to all generously and ungrudgingly—and it will be given to him"* (James 1:5). We don't need to scrounge up wisdom on our own because God's wisdom is available to us; we need only to ask.

If someone has come to mind while you read the stories of Saul and Jonathan, don't dismiss the thought. Instead allow God to shine His light on that corner of Your heart and redeem it for His glory. Then, through the power of Christ living in you, may you live out James 3:13: *"Who among you is wise and understanding? By his good conduct he should show that his works are done in the gentleness that comes from wisdom."*

EXTRA VERSES FOR STUDY OR PRAYER

James 3:13–18

VERSE OF THE DAY

But the wisdom from above is first pure, then peace-loving, gentle, compliant, full of mercy and good fruits, unwavering, without pretense.
—James 3:17

PRAYER

Jesus, forgive me for the times I've let bitter envy and selfish ambition rule in my heart. I know now that this is not from You because jealousy doesn't bring about the kind of flourishing that You desire for me. Please give me Your wisdom—the kind that is pure, peace-loving, gentle, compliant, full of mercy and good fruits, unwavering, and without pretense. As I grow in Your wisdom, may my life look different from the world. In Jesus's name, amen.

THINK

PRAY

PRAISE

TO-DO

PRAYER LIST

QUESTIONS FOR DEEPER REFLECTION

1. Invite God to open the eyes of your heart to a person you've been jealous of. Has the jealousy caused you to be harsh with them, whether in your heart or out loud?

2. Bring the jealousy to God, confessing and repenting. Then thank God for the blessings He's given that person.

DAY 26

GENTLENESS AND HUMILITY

Therefore I, the prisoner in the Lord,
urge you to walk worthy of the calling you have received,
with all humility and gentleness, with patience, bearing with
one another in love, making every effort to keep the unity of the
Spirit through the bond of peace.
—Ephesians 4:1–3

Michelle is one of the bravest people I know: she writes about race and culture online. Talking about such an often-divisive issue is a great way to get dumped on by all kinds of outraged people. But in the middle of it all, Michelle maintains a deep sense of grace and gentleness that makes her writing a beacon of hope and unity in a dark corner of the Internet. She lives out the calling Paul describes in Ephesians 4:1–3.

Unfortunately, when she began to promote grace and gentleness, Michelle started getting less traction than she did when she was being more polarizing. Specifically, her Instagram feed received far less attention than it did when she was encouraging people to take sides and be divisive. Polarizing content gives us an enemy to hate. Outrage is encouraged and rewarded, not just online, but in our world. Michelle receives more "likes" when she is ungentle or when she creates the kind of content that nurtures outrage in her followers. But she felt called to move toward posting content that came from a more gracious place. It doesn't earn her as many hearts and thumbs-up, but it shows a spiritual maturity that so many Christians lack.

SOMETHING TO THINK ABOUT

Gentleness comes from an attitude of humility. When we're humble toward God, trusting that He knows all things (and we don't) and we submit to His will, we'll be less anxious and afraid, which allows us to extend gentleness to others. But just as important is humility toward others. When I remember that I don't have all the answers and that I haven't lived anyone's life but mine, I'm able to give someone who hurt me the benefit of the doubt instead of assuming they're intentionally trying to cause me pain.

This interconnection between humility and gentleness resonates deeply with the race and culture conversation. Although we have many diverse experiences and cultures, as Christians, we are *"one body and one Spirit—just as you were called to one hope at your calling—one Lord, one faith, one baptism, one God and Father of all, who is above all and through all and in all"* (Ephesians 4:4–6). If we, as the body of Christ, can't treat each other with gentleness, it's no wonder the world looks at us and sees a very dysfunctional, bickering family that can't be trusted with problems beyond their own internal issues.

What does it actually look like to allow humility to lead us to gentleness? Proverbs 21:2 gives us a clue: *"All a person's ways seem right to him, but the LORD weighs hearts."* Even when I am convinced I'm right and someone else is wrong, I need to remember that only God knows the full truth, and He is weighing my heart. I need to acknowledge that I don't know everything and I might be wrong sometimes (or maybe often). This is a terrifying but courageous leap of faith, and when we take it, we'll find the Holy Spirit jumping with us, holding us tight.

Leadership coach Michelle Ami Reyes says:

> First, we must express our opinions with humility. Even if we are 100% right in our thinking, if we lord our opinion over

> others, what good does that do? Second, we must be willing to adapt our strong opinions. There is always the possibility that we're missing some part of the bigger picture. Or that our opinion is just one way forward, and perhaps not the best for someone else. There's also the possibility that our opinion is preventing us from truly hearing another person's heart.[24]

Are you ready to walk worthy of the calling you have received? Then it's time to invite God's Spirit to help you grow in humility so you can truly hear the hearts of those around you.

EXTRA VERSES FOR STUDY OR PRAYER

Micah 6:8; Ephesians 4:1–16; Colossians 3:12–17

VERSE OF THE DAY

Therefore I, the prisoner in the Lord, urge you to walk worthy of the calling you have received, with all humility and gentleness, with patience, bearing with one another in love, making every effort to keep the unity of the Spirit through the bond of peace.

—Ephesians 4:1–3

PRAYER

God, I confess that I don't know it all and that I might be wrong about a lot of things. Where I'm holding opinions too closely, help me to let go and listen in humility and gentleness to others. Help me to have patience and bear with those around me in the love that only You can provide. Give me courage to make every effort to keep the unity of the Spirit through the bond of peace. In Jesus's name, amen.

24. Dr. Michelle Ami Reyes, "Let's Make Our Opinions More Adaptable in 2024," *(in)courage* podcast, December 29, 2023, www.incourage.me/2023/12/lets-make-our-opinions-more-adaptable-in-2024.html.

THINK

PRAY

PRAISE

TO-DO

PRAYER LIST

QUESTIONS FOR DEEPER REFLECTION

1. Describe a situation in which you now realize you lacked humility, and as a result, you also lacked gentleness. Give this to God in prayer.

2. The best way to move into a posture of humility toward others is to listen to their stories. Name a person you often find yourself disagreeing with. How can you truly listen to their story or their heart today?

DAY 27

GENTLENESS AND ANGER

My dear brothers and sisters, understand this: Everyone should be quick to listen, slow to speak, and slow to anger, for human anger does not accomplish God's righteousness.

—James 1:19–20

In the TV show, *The Chosen*, the actors portray a scene that sums up James 1:19–20 perfectly. James and John walk up to Jesus, who stands near a trail in Samaria. Some Samaritans pass by and Jesus greets them politely. The Samaritans react with disgust, chucking rocks and spitting on the trio. Jesus holds the irate brothers back with his arms while they throw insults at the departing group. John fumes, "They deserve to have bolts of lightning rain down and incinerate them!"

"Yes! Fire from the heavens," adds James.

The two disciples know Jesus can do this and that He's given them authority to do the same. "Say the word," John demands, "and it will happen."

Instead of rebuking the Samaritans, Jesus rebukes His outraged disciples. "It's the message, the truth that we're giving them. And you're going to get in the way of that because a few people from a region you don't like were mean to you. That they're not worthy? What, you're so much better? You're more worthy? Well, let me tell you something: you're not. That's the whole point." While this is a screenwriter's depiction of this incident and Jesus's rebuke in Luke 9:52–55, it definitely gets to the heart of Jesus's message.[25]

The disciples seem to have had a hard time digesting this message of grace. On the night Jesus was arrested, Peter drew his sword and cut off the ear of the high priest's servant. In response, Jesus rebuked His disciples again. *"Put your sword back in its place because all who take up the sword will perish by the sword"* (Matthew 26:52). He then proceeded to heal the servant's ear (see Luke 22:51) and go with His accusers.

Rather than trying to address the issue of the Samaritans or the enemy soldiers in the moment, Jesus trusted His Father's plan for dealing with His enemies. He knew that reactionary, violent anger never accomplishes God's righteousness. There are moments in the Bible when we see Jesus angry, but they're always toward people like the Pharisees or those who weren't extending grace and compassion to others. In *A Gentle Answer,* Scott Sauls says, "Sometimes Jesus puts us in our place—not in spite of the fact that he loves us, but *because* he loves us."[26] That's the only kind of anger compatible with gentleness.

SOMETHING TO THINK ABOUT

In the Sermon on the Mount, Jesus says:

> *But I tell you, everyone who is angry with his brother or sister will be subject to judgment. Whoever insults his brother or sister will be subject to the court. Whoever says, "You fool!" will be subject to hellfire.* —Matthew 5:22

What is the difference between the kind of anger that accomplishes God's righteousness and the kind that Jesus warns against? James gives us a pretty cut-and-dried answer in James 1:20: *"Human*

25. *The Chosen,* "Thunder," season 2, episode 1. Directed by Dallas Jenkins. Written by Dallas Jenkins, Tyler Thompson, and Ryan Swanson. Amazon Prime; thechosen.tv, 2022–Present. "The Sons of Thunder are Born" (The Chosen Scene), youtu.be/enwt-3kQsu4?si=5meW9Ae2f3XHlzdV.

26. Sauls, *A Gentle Answer,* 105.

anger does not accomplish God's righteousness." Human anger is the problem because it comes from fear, jealousy, pride, and a desire for control. Often harsh and violent, human anger is wrong because it's self-righteous. The world may see some of the expressions of anger as a show of strength, but the Bible describes them either as imperfect responses, weakness, or sin.

If human anger is the problem, can we ever exhibit godly anger? In the Old Testament, God is often angry when His people are disobedient, when they hurt others, and when they practice witchcraft. God normally deals with these issues Himself. However, 1 Samuel 11 recounts a time when the Holy Spirit came on Saul in anger. An enemy king had laid siege to an Israelite city, threatening to gouge out the right eyes of every single resident. The people of the city sent pleas for help all throughout Israel. When Saul heard about this, *"the Spirit of God suddenly came powerfully on him, and his anger burned furiously"* (verse 6). Saul galvanized the people of Israel to work as a team, and they defeated the enemy. In this case, God's anger was channeled by His chosen vessel. So, yes, we can exhibit godly anger ... sometimes. However, while anger may sometimes be appropriate, it's never approved in the Bible as a lifestyle.

Together, let's commit to doing what Paul commands in Colossians 3:8: *"But now, put away all the following: anger, wrath, malice, slander, and filthy language from your mouth."* We put it away in the power of the Holy Spirit, allowing Him to work in our hearts to help us become quick to listen, slow to speak, and slow to anger.

EXTRA VERSES FOR STUDY OR PRAYER

Ephesians 4:31–32; Colossians 3:8; 1 Timothy 2:8

VERSE OF THE DAY

My dear brothers and sisters, understand this: Everyone should be quick to listen, slow to speak, and slow to anger, for human anger does not accomplish God's righteousness.

—James 1:19–20

PRAYER

Jesus, I've not always been quick to listen, slow to speak, or slow to anger, and my human anger has never accomplished Your righteousness. Please give me the ability and desire to hold back my anger and to choose listening over speaking, following Your way of gentleness. In Jesus's name, amen.

THINK

PRAY

PRAISE

TO-DO

PRAYER LIST

QUESTIONS FOR DEEPER REFLECTION

1. Think back to a recent time when you became angry. Do you think it was God's anger or your own?

2. What triggers your anger? Invite God to speak as you journal your answers, allowing Him to reveal the motivations behind your anger. Are there some things you need to change in order to avoid those triggers?

DAY 28

GENTLENESS AND JUSTICE

A ruler can be persuaded through patience, and a gentle tongue can break a bone.
—Proverbs 25:15

In the New Testament, we often see Jesus's gentleness toward the vulnerable leading Him into confrontation with their oppressors. However, those He confronted were rarely the people His original followers expected Jesus to oppose. Just like the first-century Jews, I would have expected the Messiah to confront the Romans for their overtaxation and unfair treatment of the Jews. But Jesus never once took the Romans to task for the way they treated His people. Rather, He focused on those who pretended to lead the people in spirit and truth but actually oppressed them with judgmental expectations. The religious leaders followed the law to the letter without offering any grace or compassion to those around them.

Once, Jesus went to the synagogue on the Sabbath and discovered a man with a withered hand. (See Mark 3:1–6.) He invited the man to come over to Him, knowing the Pharisees were watching Him closely to see if He'd break any Sabbath laws because they cared more about those than about the man. Jesus became angry and "*was grieved at the hardness of their hearts*" (verse 5). He commanded the man to stretch out his hand, which was immediately restored. Jesus does get angry, but as Scott Sauls notes, "He shows that it is possible to lose our cool without losing our character. Sometimes anger, when released from a place of health and love, is a furious force that accomplishes constructive and life-giving outcomes."[27]

Gentleness often requires us to be assertive, but not to assert our personal agendas. We can be strong and assertive while remaining gentle when we leverage power to help others instead of ourselves. Gentle justice fights for the vulnerable without making someone else vulnerable. Gentle justice is motivated by love and looks like patience. It can be harnessed to destroy evil and protect the good. It fights to oppose the evil, not the person. Like Jesus, who is both the conquering Lion and the sacrificial Lamb, it's possible for assertiveness and gentleness to be two sides of the same coin, complementing each other and finishing each other off. They're not mutually exclusive. In His gentleness, Jesus extends both comfort and justice to us, and as Christians, we ought to do the same for others, especially when people are being hurt by religious leaders.

SOMETHING TO THINK ABOUT

How can we actively fight for justice while still displaying the fruit of gentleness in our words and actions? An author for one of my favorite prayer apps wrote, "I must not fast, pray, or do justice in order to inflate my own sense of piety and weaponize my understandings against others. The fast that sets the captive free requires more than external action, it requires the rending of my heart, the guarding of my mouth, and the laying down of my life."[28] The author is referring to Isaiah 58:1–6 in which God expresses frustration with those who fast and deny themselves for God but don't do anything to help His people. Gentle justice doesn't mean we give lip-service to justice and sit back meekly. Instead, God asks us to hold back harshness with one hand and hold out help with the other:

> *If you get rid of the yoke among you, the finger-pointing and malicious speaking, and if you offer yourself to the hungry, and*

27. Sauls, *A Gentle Answer*, 106.

28. Lectio 365, produced by 24-7 Prayer, morning prayer for September 1, 2023, lectio365.com.

> *satisfy the afflicted one, then your light will shine in the darkness, and your night will be like noonday.* —Isaiah 58:9–10

As Proverbs 25:15 points out, gentleness doesn't mean being wimpy, scared, or sitting back to watch a problem play itself out. Rather, *"a gentle tongue can break a bone."* Difficult tasks and world-changing justice can be accomplished through patience, gentleness, and a willingness to be assertive to put others first.

EXTRA VERSES FOR STUDY OR PRAYER

Second Corinthians 1:3–4

VERSE OF THE DAY

> *A ruler can be persuaded through patience, and a gentle tongue can break a bone.* —Proverbs 25:15

PRAYER

Jesus, thanks for Your example of fighting for justice by dying on the cross and coming back to life again. Help me not to turn away from the pain in the world; instead, break my heart for the things that break Your heart. Teach me to walk in Your ways rather than mine. And if I get a chance to talk to a ruler who needs to change, help me to practice persuasion through patience and gentleness instead of trying to ram my opinions through by force. In Jesus's name, amen.

THINK

PRAY

PRAISE

TO-DO

PRAYER LIST

QUESTIONS FOR DEEPER REFLECTION

1. What issue in the world bothers you a lot because of the harm experienced by someone vulnerable? How might God be inviting you to participate in the fight for justice while still showing gentleness?

2. In this area, how could you practice holding back harshness while holding out help at the same time?

DAY 29

GENTLENESS AND BEAUTY

Don't let your beauty consist of outward things like elaborate hairstyles and wearing gold jewelry or fine clothes, but rather what is inside the heart—the imperishable quality of a gentle and quiet spirit, which is of great worth in God's sight. For in the past, the holy women who put their hope in God also adorned themselves in this way.

—1 Peter 3:3–5

Apparently makeup companies consider me old because all my Instagram ads are about makeup for aging women. "This foundation is perfect for aging skin," boasts the perfectly-coiffed woman, her own aging skin glowing and wrinkle-free. "This shampoo is medically-proven to turn back the time on gray hair," says a bald man in a lab coat. Why does it seem that the entire Western world is terrified of gray hair and facial wrinkles?

In his letter to Christians around the Roman world, Peter admonished women to stop stressing about outer beauty and start caring more about what was in their hearts. When I was a teenager, I chopped my hair short because I thought my longer hair was making me vain, but I'm not convinced this verse means we all need to burn our bras and toss our makeup. There are several times in Scripture when women are adorned beautifully and God doesn't assign moral value to their clothing. (See, for example, Genesis 24:22; Esther 5:1;

Proverbs 31:22.) There are even times when Israel is described as God's precious, bejeweled bride. (See Isaiah 62:3–5; Ezekiel 16:10–13.) It's not the jewelry, clothes, or hairstyles that are the problem, but rather what they reveal about our hearts. Does my identity lie in how I look? Do I feel less valued when I'm not wearing stylish clothes? Do I judge others for having sagging eyes or frizzy hair? Therein lies the problem: not with the outer presentation but with the heart.

Peter invites women to have *"the imperishable quality of a gentle and quiet spirit"* (1 Peter 3:4). It's important to note that Peter never says our personalities should be gentle and quiet. Having a gentle and quiet spirit doesn't mean I need to whisper, keep my opinions to myself, or walk on eggshells. As discussed on day 12, gentleness is about crucifying my ungodly passions, not changing my God-given personality. As Twyla Franz points out, "A gentle spirit runs counter to what culture celebrates: independence and rightness. Self-made success. Goal setting and exponential growing. We buy into the lie that we don't need God. But gentleness is an invitation to humility ... It encourages us to move aside and let God be big."[29]

If my ungodly passions lead me to value independence over God-reliance, rightness over humility, self-made success over God-given desires, they need to be crucified with Christ. Likewise, if my godly passions include obsessing over clothes or considering my appearance to be more important than loving others, they also need to be crucified with Christ so Christ can live in me.

This is why a gentle and quiet spirit is *"of great worth in God's sight"* (1 Peter 3:4). It means we've chosen a life with Him rather than a life dedicated to ourselves. Consider the holy women described in this Scripture and compare them to the haughty, beautified women of Jerusalem.

> *The Lord also says: Because the daughters of Zion are haughty, walking with heads held high and seductive eyes, prancing along, jingling their ankle bracelets, the Lord will put scabs on the heads*

29. Twyla Franz, "The Truth About Gentleness Most People Miss," June 13, 2023, twylafranz.com/the-truth-about-gentleness-most-people-miss.

> *of the daughters of Zion, and the* Lord *will shave their foreheads bare. On that day the Lord will strip their finery … Instead of perfume there will be a stench; instead of a belt, a rope; instead of beautifully styled hair, baldness; instead of fine clothes, sackcloth; instead of beauty, branding.* —Isaiah 3:16–18, 24

God wasn't angry because they were beautiful but because they were proud, and their adornment was a physical manifestation of their pride. Just like the women of Sodom, they tried to use physical beauty to cover up their rotting hearts.

> *Now this was the iniquity of your sister Sodom: She and her daughters had pride, plenty of food, and comfortable security, but didn't support the poor and needy.* —Ezekiel 16:49

SOMETHING TO THINK ABOUT

Peter's letter says having a gentle and quiet spirit gives a woman an imperishable quality; 1 Peter 3:4 (NIV) calls it *"unfading beauty."* This is the kind of beauty that doesn't wrinkle or turn to gray. It doesn't require cosmetic surgery, but does require that we let God do surgery in our hearts. The amazing part is that it's free and only gets more beautiful with age, as we continue to grow in gentleness. (No bald men in lab coats required!)

EXTRA VERSES FOR STUDY OR PRAYER

First Samuel 16:7; Proverbs 31:30

VERSE OF THE DAY

> *Don't let your beauty consist of outward things like elaborate hairstyles and wearing gold jewelry or fine clothes, but rather what is inside the heart—the imperishable quality of a gentle and quiet spirit, which is of great worth in God's sight. For in the past, the holy women who put their hope in God also adorned themselves in this way.* —1 Peter 3:3–5

PRAYER

Jesus, please forgive me for the times I've cared more about my appearance than about my heart. Please teach me to put less stock in outward things and focus more on what's inside my heart. Show me what it means for me to have a gentle and quiet spirit. In Jesus's name, amen.

THINK

PRAY

PRAISE

TO-DO

PRAYER LIST

QUESTIONS FOR DEEPER REFLECTION

1. Is there any aspect of your physical appearance that you've felt prideful over? Or is there an aspect of your appearance that you're unhappy with? Tell God about it as you reflect on today's verse.

2. Is there an aspect of your skincare routine, clothing, or hairstyling that needs to change in light of God's gentleness and care for the vulnerable?

DAY 30

GENTLENESS AND WARFARE

His divine power has given us everything required for life and godliness through the knowledge of him who called us by his own glory and goodness.
—2 Peter 1:3

My son rushed to the front door every few hours, flinging it open with anticipation and then closing it glumly. He had ordered something online and was increasingly frustrated that he had to wait for days for its arrival. We live in a society where so many things happen instantly, we get frustrated anytime we have to wait.

We can be similarly frustrated when waiting for spiritual growth. Maybe you wish you'd changed more through this journal. Or perhaps you *have* changed, but people have started to take advantage of your gentleness. It's so easy to get discouraged and whisper into the darkness, "Is it really worth walking this road of gentleness? What am I getting out of it?" Our enemy wants us to think that following Christ's way of gentleness isn't worth the effort or that we can't win against our sinful nature. But 2 Peter 1:3 says Jesus's "*divine power has given us everything*" we need "*for life and godliness.*" We don't have to wait by the door for God to drop off a package; He's already given it to us. Christ has won the victory over sin and death, and we need merely to stand in that truth. We get discouraged because we have an enemy who lies. Watchman Nee once said, "Satan's primary objective is not to get us to sin, but simply to make it easy for us to do so by getting us off the ground of perfect triumph onto which the Lord has brought us."[30]

Romans 8:37 says, "*We are more than conquerors,*" but our enemy wants us to act like victims. We live in the victory won by Christ but often step off the ground of triumph. We've been given the gift of salvation but do our best to try to *earn* it. We hold the sword of the Spirit but forget to wield it.

In our struggle against evil, against harshness and human anger, against pride and quarreling and selfishness, we don't need to fight for victory. Jesus already did that when He died, rose again, and ascended to sit at the right hand of God the Father. The battle is already won, so we get to fight *from* victory, not *for* victory.

But how do we do this? In 2 Chronicles 20, the people of Judah were horrified to discover an enormous army marching toward them. King Jehoshaphat led a prayer assembly, which he began by praising God for giving them the land in the first place. He reminded God (and everyone listening) that God had already given them the victory. The land was theirs, and they simply looked to their heavenly King for help in keeping it. As he paused, the Spirit of God spoke through the prophet Jahaziel:

> *This is what the* Lord *says: "Do not be afraid or discouraged because of this vast number, for the battle is not yours, but God's. Tomorrow, go down against them. You will see them coming up the Ascent of Ziz, and you will find them at the end of the valley facing the Wilderness of Jeruel. You do not have to fight this battle. Position yourselves, stand still, and see the salvation of the* Lord*."*
>
> —2 Chronicles 20:15–17

On the way to meet the enemy the next morning, King Jehoshaphat appointed some people to walk in front of the army, singing praises to God. "*The moment they began their shouts and praises*" (verse 22), their enemies began to fight among themselves. When the

30. Nee, *Sit, Walk, Stand*, 58.

people of Judah came to the place where the enemies' army had been, all they saw were dead bodies, ready for plunder.

SOMETHING TO THINK ABOUT

There are many other moments in the Bible when God fights on behalf of His people, requiring only that they get into position, *"stand still, and see the salvation of the Lord"* (2 Chronicles 20:17). Through them, we can see the posture we need to adopt. Rather than waiting for gentleness, pleading for it, or being depressed over our lack of it, we need to focus our hearts on God, praising Him for the victory He's already won. We can strive less and praise more. And in our praises, we'll *"be strengthened by the Lord and by his vast strength"* (Ephesians 6:10). With the armor of God taken up and worn, we will be able to stand in the victory Christ has already won against the darkness.

EXTRA VERSES FOR STUDY OR PRAYER

Ephesians 6:10–17; Colossians 3:15–17

VERSE OF THE DAY

His divine power has given us everything required for life and godliness through the knowledge of him who called us by his own glory and goodness. —2 Peter 1:3

PRAYER

Jesus, I praise You. You called me by Your own glory and goodness, not mine. In Your divine power, You have given me everything I need for life and godliness. Thank You for Your great and precious promises and that through them, I might share in Your nature, becoming perfect as my heavenly Father is perfect, through the power of Your Spirit living in me. In Jesus's victorious name, amen.

THINK

PRAY

PRAISE

TO-DO

PRAYER LIST

QUESTIONS FOR DEEPER REFLECTION

1. How has your understanding of gentleness changed over the course of this prayer journal? In what area do you still need to grow? How does it help to know that God has already won the victory over sin in every area of your life?

2. Spend some time praising God for who He and what He's already doing in your life.

ABOUT THE AUTHOR

Christie Thomas was a children's ministries director for over a decade and is now a homeschool mom and family discipleship coach to parents who need equipping, support, and encouragement.

She is also a member of the leadership team for the Daughters First Retreat at Glen Eyrie, Colorado Springs.

Christie believes that every Christian parent can confidently nurture deep faith in their children through little habits that add up over time. Her ministry, Little Shoots Deep Roots, creates award-winning books and resources to help families cultivate faith-filled moments.

Christie received her bachelor's degree from the University of Alberta. She lives with her husband and three boys in Alberta, Canada.